"Judy G ... t place on "the otl ... er remembrance (... ctus spine, honest a ... rough the desert sl ... met along the way. ... sdom and admirat ... e for anyone whc ... d another way of l

...he Moon:

"Judy Gc ... and mind of Baja's ... l through their per ... ives north of the b(

...lifornia

"In *The* ... her own, highly p ... d experienced in ... lete with otherfoll ... o participate, and find that we have been handed a new set of keys to our lives."

—Harry W. Crosby, author of:
The Cave Paintings of Baja California
Antigua California
The King's Highway in Baja California
Last of the Californios

"Told with warmth and love, Judy Goldstein Botello's story is a gentle and enjoyable first step for those who wish to understand both Baja California and what it means to live on the border. Judy Goldstein Botello crosses the border in a way that allows other outsiders to follow her through acceptance, love, and understanding."

—Tamara Collins, professor of Crosscultural Education,
College of Education, San Diego State University

The Other Side

Journeys in Baja California

Written by

Judy Goldstein Botello

SUNBELT PUBLICATIONS
San Diego, California

Copyright © 1998 by Sunbelt Publications, Inc.

ınbelt Publications, Inc.

in any form without
ɔts for review or academic
) Sunbelt Publications, Inc.
her:

Sunbelt Publications, Inc.
P.O. Box 191126
San Diego, CA 92159-1126
(619) 258-4911 (619)258-4916 fax

01 00 99 98   5 4 3 2 1

Library of Congress Cataloging-in-Publication Data

Botello, Judy Goldstein. 1943-
   The Other Side: Journeys in Baja California / written by Judy
Goldstein Botello.

              p.   cm. — (Sunbelt Publications, Inc.)

   ISBN 0-932653-25-1
   First Edition 1998.
   1. Baja California (Mexico) -- Description and Travel. 2. Baja
California (Mexico)-- Social life and customs. 3. Botello, Judy,
1943- .
   I. Title.

F1246.B68   1998
917.2'20483—dc21   98-22892
                                                 CIP

Photo Credits:
Front cover photo: Photodisc Copyright 1998
Back cover photo: Janet Wikler

para Victor

Baja California

Tijuana
Ensenada
Ejido Eréndira

El Rosario
Cataviña
Punta Cono
Bahía de Los Angeles
La Sierra de San Francisco
San Ignacio
Mulegé
Bahía Concepción

San José del Cabo

N
W   E
S

CONTENTS

Author's Note

This book covers a decade and a half, from 1978 to 1993, a time of relative innocence in the life of Baja California and in my own life as well. We came of age together, Baja and I, and this is the record of our adventures along the way.

Those who traveled the Baja peninsula during those peaceful years will understand my desire to capture an era: people and places that now live only in our hearts and in our stories. And those who travel that other road—the one that leads to the soul's desert places—will understand why today, more than ever, we need the experience of the other side. These tales are for all those fellow travelers. May the journey never end.

ACKNOWLEDGMENTS

This is not a work of fiction. However, in a few cases people's names and locations have been changed to protect their privacy.

I want to thank all those whose encouragement has sustained me through this project's long gestation: my sister Janet Wikler who believed in me even when I didn't; my fellow scribblers Karen Moreland, John McKiernan and James Williams, all of whom provided valuable suggestions along with unconditional support; and Diana Lindsay whose enthusiasm for the book rekindled my own when it began to flag. My long-time comrade Cathy Granett has been my most loyal fan over more years than either of us can remember.

Harry Crosby, Gene Kira, and Luis Urrea have been my role models both as writers and as Baja aficionados. All three were very generous with their time and their considerable wisdom.

Dan Hammer's editorial advice has been invaluable, and especially precious as it came mixed with large doses of encouragement. Shelley Hammer, above all people, first opened my eyes and my heart to Baja's magic.

It would be impossible to adequately thank the people of Baja California for all they teach me and all they give me. With their characteristic tolerance and good humor, they continue to receive me into their lives; they have long since become part of my own. *Muchísimas gracias por todo.*

JGB

Prologue

About borders, there is this: They define us as well as divide us. Whether a political line between nations or a psychological line between lovers, every border seems, at first glance, to define who we are in terms of who we are not. But it is only when we enter the threshold region between the self and the other that we encounter the real defining power of borders; for in that region the borderline shifts and blurs—what seemed a clear duality becomes a multifaceted unity. Crossing over becomes a kind of odyssey, an adventure not into the other, but rather into new landscapes of the self.

Mexicans understand this concept of borders. An American may say, "I crossed the border this morning," connoting an act fixed in space and time. But a Mexican will say, "*me voy pa'el otro lado,*" "I'm going over to the other side," suggesting a process rather than a discrete act—an entire shift of consciousness, a journey into another reality.

There are those who never encounter the other side. But for those who do, the adventure can begin in many ways: with a love affair, a casual weekend vacation, or a chance meeting in a bar. For me, it began with music . . .

The Other Side

Journeys in Baja California

Tijuana

Voz de la guitarra mía
al despertar la mañana
quiere cantar la alegría
de mi tierra mexicana.

The voice of my guitar
with the wakening day
longs to sing the joy
of my Mexican land.

—Chucho Monge, "México Lindo"

It started with guitars in the night. Deep in sleep, I felt the round, bright chords tossed against my window like little golden apples. Then I heard soft male laughter and a familiar tenor voice singing: "*Abre el balcón y el corazón*," "open your balcony and your heart." I came awake in the darkness, smiling. The closest thing to a balcony in my southern California bungalow was a concrete patio; but I switched on my bedside light, padded across the carpet, and slid open the glass door. If I had imagined a serenade before that night, I would have seen it in grainy black-and-white: a balcony, a young girl in white chiffon, a handsome swain below on one knee, his sombrero over his heart. But the woman who now stood at the patio door wrapped in a red flannel bathrobe was a thirty-four-year-old divorced mother of two young children, and the serenaders were two tipsy friends in ski jackets, both too portly to balance on one knee. It didn't look anything like the old movies, but in my memory that night glows with an amber light, soft and warm, as if seen through a tinted lens, a diffusing filter. Carlos and Jorge came in from the chilly air and sat on the end of my bed drinking coffee and singing in Spanish of moonlit lakes and fishermen, of broken hearts and tequila. I reclined on the faded quilt, periodically hissing "shhh" when I remembered that my kids were sleeping in the next room. After I went to the kitchen for a second round of coffee and a bottle of Kahlúa, I pulled my old guitar out from under the bed and tried to tune it to theirs. The strings were brittle and stiff and almost impossible to tune; the E string snapped when I wound it too tight. The guitar, cheap when I had bought it twenty years before, wore the scratches and cracks of my restless youth and the dust of a silent decade. One of the hinges had come off the plastic case; inside were miscellaneous sheets of songs with chord notations, some in my own writing. "Mr. Tambourine Man" stared up at me from where a young woman's careless hand had flung him years ago, when the music stopped. Carlos grinned, mischievous as a boy. "We have to get you a new guitar," he said. "I'm going to teach you some *good* songs!"

Carlos and Jorge had both come to the U.S. from central Mexico in their twenties, and had met one another at one of our local community colleges where they both taught Spanish. After Jorge's wife left him for an American accountant, he and Carlos became roommates, sharing the expenses of Jorge's little house in town. When I found myself single again and moved into the house across the street from them, they offered to help carry my heavy sofa bed in from the moving van. My next-door neighbor, Barbara, warned me against them. She and I were sipping ice tea by her pool, which she had graciously made available to me and to my cranky children one hot July evening that first summer. "You know these Mexican men . . . " she said in a conspiratorial tone. In fact, I didn't know Mexican men at all, having socialized for the past ten years exclusively with my husband's friends, most of whom were East Coast transplants like us. But I didn't want Barbara to think me naive, so I nodded knowingly, crunching on a corn chip to hide my ignorance. Barbara tipped back her lawn chair, stretching her long tennis-tanned legs. "Well," she yawned, "you just watch yourself with them. I wouldn't trust them if I were you."

Despite Barbara's concerns, when The Mexicans (as they were known on our street) invited me to join them for a backyard barbecue the next Saturday, I accepted. My kids were with their dad for the weekend, and my biggest plan for the day had been to unpack my spice jars and arrange them in alphabetical order. A little social life sounded a lot better, so I combed my hair, put on some lipstick, and went over.

The garage door was open, and there was a hot ping-pong tournament going on as I walked by. Letting myself into the house through the front door, I followed the sound of voices to the kitchen, where a bilingual assembly line buzzed at the counter as chopped tomatoes and chiles somehow collected themselves in clay bowls amid the cheerful chaos. The fragrance of corn tortillas drifted in through the open window and drew me out to the patio, where Carlos and Jorge presided over a brick barbecue. They waved when they saw me, and Carlos pulled a chunk of *carne asada* off the grill, wrapped it in a hot tortilla, and popped it into my mouth. "Try it, you'll like it!" he said. And I did.

Later, as dusk began to fall, the guitars came out. Carlos and Jorge sang the old romantic Mexican songs of their youth. Bob Shaffer, a long-limbed rancher with thinning blond hair and a grizzled beard, sang the old folk songs of his youth and mine. By the time I went home, he and I had managed a pretty fair rendition of "Feelin' Groovy." As I sank into sleep, the music drifted across the summer night and settled around me softly like a bright net floating on dark water.

After that evening I invited Carlos and Jorge over once on a Sunday morning for lox and bagels, which they had never tasted before. We joked about opening a restaurant called "Carlos Goldstein's" where we would serve lox tacos and jalapeño bagels. But as summer faded into autumn and then winter, my life slid along its narrow groove, carrying me predictably from my office to my kids' soccer practices to my kitchen table, where dinner gave way to homework and then to bills and paperwork. I saw little of my neighbors and almost forgot about the musical summer evening. Then came that cold Saturday night in January when The Mexicans—homesick, perhaps, or just drunk—crossed over to my side of the street and awoke me with a serenade. A week later, I crossed the border for the first time.

Carlos called me on Friday.

"We're going to Sevillano's tomorrow," he said. "Jorge's *requinto* guitar is being repaired, and Bob wants to order a new flamenco. Want to come?"

"What's Sevillano's?" I asked dubiously.

"Miguel Sevillano. He's a guitar maker in Tijuana. We all have Sevillano guitars. Didn't you notice the labels? C'mon, you'll enjoy it. Who knows? You might end up with a Sevillano guitar, too!"

"I don't know," I stalled. "My kids are gone and I was going to clean out my cupboards . . . "

"Don't give me that!" Carlos's laugh was warm, deep in his chest. "I'll pick you up at 9:00 *mañana*."

At 9:35 the next morning I allowed myself to peek out my front window, wondering if I had imagined the invitation. The garage door across the street was still closed, but Bob's pickup truck was parked at the curb. I resisted the urge to call or go over. At 9:55 I heard the unmistakable sound of a Volkswagen engine outside and saw Carlos's blue van in my driveway. "What took you so long?" he grinned as I climbed in. I shot him an annoyed look and settled down next to Bob and his wife Sue, a tall, comfortably soft woman whom I had met at the barbecue and who greeted me like an old friend. Jorge rode shotgun, downing Budweisers from the cooler at his feet and laughing amiably at Bob's Peace Corps stories, all of which he had obviously heard before. The van rattled onto the freeway and headed south.

At the San Diego/Tijuana border the wide, straight lanes of Interstate 5 come to an abrupt halt; indeed, all linearity seems to end. The blue van wove in and out of traffic that looked as though it had no direction at all, or all directions at once. Cars cut randomly in and out of what would have been our lane, had there been any lanes.

"Is it always like this?" I clutched Sue's arm.

"No." She gave my hand a pat. "Sometimes it's really scary!" A gigantic bronze Cuauhtémoc suddenly loomed directly in front of us, headdress glinting in the windshield. We swerved around him and maneuvered through the traffic circle, continuing south along the road whose only name—as far as anyone knows—is "The Old Road to Ensenada." Finally we pulled over to what would have been the shoulder—had there been any shoulders—in front of a pharmacy and a tire shop.

"Where are we?" I asked. "Aren't we going to a guitar store?"

"We are." Carlos slid open the van's side door and I stepped out.

Then I saw the sign: GUITARRAS, in hand-printed letters, so faded that it almost disappeared between the newer, larger FARMACIA and LLANTAS signs that flanked it. It was carved in the shape of a guitar and jutted out from a block wall over a narrow doorway. Carlos entered, and we all followed.

The floor space in the rectangular room was almost completely filled by a rough wooden workbench, covered with sawdust and hung with a few simple hand-tools: a vice, a saw, an awl. Bending over the workbench with his back to the door was a small, dark figure. He appeared to be filing something with intense concentration and did not respond immediately when we went in. Carlos called out, "Don Miguel!" The man turned slowly, straightening up and wiping his hands on his long brown apron. When he saw Carlos and Jorge, his smooth face opened into a broad grin, and he embraced them both amid soft exclamations of greeting.

"You remember Bob," said Jorge. Sevillano shook Bob's hand, then embraced him, too.

"*¿Cómo estás, Roberto?*" he inquired. "*¿Y cómo está la guitarra?*"

"And this is Bob's wife Susana, and our friend Judy."

Sevillano shook hands gravely with Sue and with me. His hand felt surprisingly large for such a slight man. The palm was callused. "*Mucho gusto, señora,*" he said, inclining his head in a subtle bow. I merely nodded, unsure of the proper response.

By that time, Bob had taken a flamenco guitar off the wall and was tuning it, one leg propped on a Corona beer carton. Sevillano disappeared into a back room and emerged with a small *requinto* guitar, which he handed to Jorge. "She is better than ever," he said. "See if you recognize her voice." Tenderly, Jorge caressed the smooth face of the guitar.

"*¡Mira!*" he breathed. "The crack is gone!" Jorge strummed a chord as Sevillano folded his arms over his chest with a confident smile. On the flamenco he had taken from the wall, Bob struck up "El Rancho Grande." Jorge joined in with his *requinto*, tentatively at first, then gathering confidence until Carlos—who had been examining the half-formed instrument on the workbench—raised his head with an exuberant "*ay yay yay yay yay yaaaay,*" and a couple of passersby stopped at the open door to listen. Sue had draped her sweater over the room's only chair and was seated on its cracked vinyl. I found a spot on Bob's Corona carton and sat down, gazing around the little shop.

The walls were hung with guitars in varying stages: a shiny new flamenco, ready to buy; an elegant classical with no strings or tuning keys; an old *requinto* whose face was scratched and dull but whose mouth sported a new mother-of-pearl rosette. Two pairs of dusty castanets dangled from a nail below a bare lightbulb. Surrounding the guitars and covering most of the wall-space were the girls: scores of pinups in provocative poses, some fresh, others a little worn. A brunette in a leopard skin décolletage leaned from a Cadillac convertible. Just below her hung a faded 8 x 10 aerial photograph of Dodger Stadium. Tacked haphazardly around Dodger Stadium were old snapshots of Little League teams, small boys staring proudly at the camera. On the back wall hung a life-sized cardboard skeleton, and around him were tacked a few Polaroids of a family wedding along with two publicity photos of Mexican guitarists and one of Goldie Hawn. On the contiguous wall, and higher than any pinup, a pink and gold Virgin of Guadalupe raised her right hand in blessing; the gothic lettering proclaimed her *Reina de México y Emperatriz de América.*

Bob had hung the flamenco back on the wall and was crouching beside Sevillano, who had pulled several thin sheets of wood from a cabinet along the floor.

"He's choosing the wood for his new guitar," Carlos explained to me. "Why don't you take a look, too? This one has a beautiful grain." He laid a fragrant sheet of rosewood over my knees, and my fingers traced the graceful swirls running through it. Jorge brought over a couple of sheets of cedar for the guitar's face, and I lingered over one with a rich golden brown color. "Like your hair," said Jorge. Sue was sorting through a drawer full of silver tuning keys, some elaborately carved, some simple. By the time Bob had finished designing and ordering his guitar, I had chosen mine down to the tiny butterflies to be inlaid around the mouth. Sevillano listened attentively as Carlos explained what I wanted. "*Muy bien,*" he said, simply.

"Is that it?" I asked Carlos. "Doesn't he need to write out an order slip? Don't I have to leave a deposit? Shouldn't I have a receipt?"

Carlos laughed. Sevillano called a small boy from the back room and sent him running out the door. A moment later the boy returned with a nylon shopping bag full of cold Coronas which he handed around the room.

"That's your receipt," said Carlos. He helped himself to one of the guitars on the wall, and Jorge played a riff on his *requinto*. They launched into "*Camino de Guanajuato*," Bob following the chords. Don Miguel leaned against his workbench and smiled benevolently while Sue and I hummed and swayed.

"*No vale nada la vida*," they sang, "Life is worth nothing!" And they sang it with such joy that I waved my Corona bottle in a spontaneous salute.

For me, the next few months were filled with music. In early February, Carlos gave me several tapes of Mexican songs he thought I would like. Chavela Vargas, he told me, made him think of me. I wasn't sure how to take that: her voice sounded like smoky rooms and candlelight, not the self-image of a lady doctor from Philadelphia. But in the privacy of my car, driving to work, I found myself singing along with her: "*No soy de aquí ni soy de allá*," "I am neither from here nor from there." In the evenings, at home, I listened to the tapes with earphones on my ears and a dictionary on my lap, trying to learn the words. The only lyrics Carlos would actually write out for me were to "*La Llorona*," a folk song of obscure origins and infinite verses. *La Llorona* is the Weeping Woman, a lady of mysterious sorrow who lives in rivers—under bridges or hidden beneath the waters—and who is either a witch or an angel, depending upon the version. After I read the words, I told Carlos that the first verse reminded me of him:

Todos me dicen El Negro, Llorona,
Negro, pero cariñoso.
Yo soy como el chile verde, Llorona,
picante, pero sabroso.

Everyone calls me the Black One, *Llorona,*
Black, but full of tenderness.
I am like the green chili, *Llorona,*
biting, but delicious.

Sometimes Carlos and Jorge would come over for supper with me and my kids, and afterward we'd all sing. Nine-year-old Cathy and five-year-old Josh loved "*De Colores*," a bright tune from César Chávez's farmworkers' movement, full of rainbows and animal sounds (The rooster sings *kiri-kiri-kiri-kiri!*) I loved "*La Bamba*," of which I understood only six words: "*Para bailar la Bamba se necesita* ... " Whatever it was one needed to dance the Bamba, I wanted some.

One night, after Cathy and Josh had gone to sleep, Carlos and Jorge sang a song I hadn't heard before, and they sang it with deep feeling rather than with their usual cheerful irreverence. "*México, lindo y querido*," they sang, "*si muero lejos de ti, que digan que estoy dormido, y que me traigan a ti.*"

"That's lovely," I said, moved by the few phrases I had caught. "What does it mean?" Carlos couldn't speak. Jorge answered.

"That's a song for all of us exiles here in *gringolandia*," he explained. "It means, 'Mexico, beautiful and beloved, if I die far from you, let them say that I'm only sleeping, and carry me back to you.'"

I wondered then what winding *caminos* had led these two men so far from their beautiful and beloved Mexico. Over the years I would be granted an occasional backward glimpse of an earnest young priest once known to local villagers as Padre Jorge. I would hear, on certain evenings, the sweet splash of a fountain in Carlos's native Aguascalientes where, he claimed, if you put your ear to the ground you could hear the heart of Mexico beating. But whenever I tried to penetrate deeper into those distances, shadows would spring up like dark vines, and I would find myself back in the eternal present tense that was, I came to realize, the natural habitat of both men.

It was late March before Carlos took Sue and Bob and me back down to Tijuana to pick up our guitars. When we crossed the border, I noticed that we took a different route than we had the first time.

"I want to show you *la frontera*." Carlos looked at me in the rear view mirror as he spoke. The border, in those days, consisted of a barbed wire fence running along the crest of a hill. To the north of the wire, a treeless field known as No Man's Land stretched out for a couple of miles to where San Diego's skyline shone like a mirage. On the south side of the wire, barefoot children peered unsmiling from shacks made of packing crates and tar paper. I thought of the comment attributed to one of Mexico's archbishops during the politically turbulent 1920s: "Poor Mexico," the archbishop had observed, "so far from God, and so close to the United States."

Bob was saying, "Those folks you see sitting there are just waiting to cross the border when it gets dark." As Carlos slowed the van, I saw that there were numerous large holes in the barbed wire where it had been cut or bent. Groups of people, many of them apparently families, clustered around the openings. They reclined on blankets or relaxed in lawn chairs. Most had coolers and baskets of food, and some played music on portable tape decks. They all faced north, but otherwise the whole scene had the air of a picnic, as if it were the most natural thing in the world to slip across an international border in the dead of night and creep across No Man's Land to safety. In fact, as I was to learn later, many crossed back and forth regularly and even developed light-hearted friendships with the border guards. Those guards—who were often on a first-name basis with their "regulars"—continually bussed the same individuals back to Tijuana only to accost them in San Diego a week later, with resigned good humor.

The van rounded a curve, and the border disappeared from view. A broad, modern boulevard, lined by fashionable shops and restaurants, swept down to the bronze statue of Cuauhtémoc. When I saw him I knew we were almost there.

It had been two months since I had ordered my guitar and my fingers were itching to strum it. Sevillano greeted us with his grave courtesy and assured us that our instruments were almost ready. When he brought mine out to show me, my spirits sagged. The guitar looked naked with its unpolished face and half-carved neck. Bob's instrument was at the same indeterminate stage of gestation. Carlos and Sue went down the street and brought back a six-pack while Bob and I tried out "Me and Bobby McGee" on a couple of classical guitars from the wall. Bob was off-key, and the beat was too slow, and my Janis Joplin imitation was a nasal whine. But Sevillano's calm, kind expression never changed as he polished a red flamenco till it shone. Then Carlos opened a beer and played "*Cielito Lindo*," which we could all sing. We toasted to Sevillano's health and promised to return soon.

"It's lunch time," Carlos announced as we turned into a narrow street, made even narrower by cars that were double-parked up and down its length. Carlos left the van in what looked to me like the middle of the street, and slipped a bill to one of the small boys who surged around us. "Mexican car insurance," he explained, grinning. On the sidewalk outside the restaurant an enormous copper pot sat on bricks over a wood fire. A mass of fragrant steam almost obscured the figure of the man who was stirring the pot with a five-foot-long wooden paddle.

"What is it?" I asked, half afraid of the answer.

"*Carnitas.*" Sue took my arm reassuringly.

I was translating in my mind: "*Carnitas.* Little meats?"

I couldn't hear her answer. Three mariachi bands blared from three corners of the restaurant; waitresses shouted orders across a counter in the front; and at long wooden tables patrons sang lustily and called out for more beer, more *carnitas.* We managed to find four empty places at one of the long tables, and within five minutes we were singing and shouting, too. I discovered that *carnitas* are succulent chunks of pork which, when wrapped in a fresh corn tortilla spread with salsa and cilantro, taste so sweet that I consumed five tacos and was licking my fingers before the word *cholesterol* even entered my mind. After we had devoured the first kilogram of meat, Carlos ordered another round of Pacifico beers, and beckoned to one of the bands. Five men approached our table. All wore tight pants, short jackets, and big mariachi sombreros. Their black costumes were festooned with silver studs. Their boots and their belts were soft leather, elaborately worked. A short, fat man played the *guitarrón*, an oversized guitar with a full, deep voice like that of its owner. The *requinto* player, small and animated, beamed and bobbed as his fingers moved like a hummingbird's wings across the strings. The trumpeter looked like Don Quixote, tall and thin and gloomy, with eyes that drooped to match his mustache. It was the guitarists with whom I fell in love, both of them: one stocky and middle-aged with salt-and-pepper hair and kind lines at the corners of his eyes, the other young and intense with long black hair and full, pouting lips.

It was the younger one who gazed insolently at me as they sang "*Ella;*" but it was the older, kinder one who nodded and smiled when, after my third beer, I belted out the chorus to "*Corazón, Corazón.*"

April came and went, and at the end of May we went back to Sevillano's. The guitars, he assured us, were almost ready. That evening we ate at the old Palacio Azteca Hotel on the top floor, overlooking the lights of Tijuana. The grizzled waiters, dignified despite missing teeth and bent frames, hovered like courtly ghosts from the 1920s when Tijuana had been the playground of Hollywood celebrities who came to gamble at the Agua Caliente racetrack and to drink in the Prohibition-free clubs. In the restaurant's dim light, a patina of old elegance seemed to cling to the worn leather seats and faded draperies. The city, spread out below us like a feast, looked glamorous, pulsating with life. The band played Latin rhythms: *bolero, danzón*. I danced with Carlos.

"You move like a gringa," he told me. "Loosen your hips!" He stepped back and demonstrated, to the amusement of Jorge who was smoking a cigarette and watching from the table. Bob and Sue threw me sympathetic glances. I tried to get back to my seat, but Carlos planted both his hands on my torso. "Let yourself go," he instructed. "Just move from the waist." I blushed and tried out a step or two, holding myself stiffly away from Carlos and watching his feet. He laughed. "Never mind," he said. He draped his arm around my shoulder, leading me back to the table. "I'll buy you a margarita." I reached for the pack of Winstons lying by Jorge's glass. He looked surprised but flicked on his lighter and held it out for me.

"I didn't know you smoked," he said.

"I don't," I answered, inhaling deeply. Through the veil of smoke, I watched the dancers. A short, bald man glided across the floor with a big brunette in a tight, electric-blue dress. He gazed at her as though she were the most beautiful woman in the world as they undulated in perfect unison, sensing each other's moves. Despite a lovely chignon and heavy make-up, the woman looked at least fifty, and her overblown flesh strained against seams and bodice. But she moved her hips with an easy sensuality, and she radiated a serene confidence in her femininity. I wriggled my buttocks a little on the chair, surreptitiously, practicing to the beat.

In June when the guitars weren't ready, we went to a bullfight.

"It isn't really a fight," said Carlos. "That's just the gringo translation, but it's wrong. In Spanish we call it a *corrida*, a running of the bulls. Or sometimes we call it *la fiesta brava*, the festival of courage."

"Does the bull ever win?" I asked. We were sitting on wooden seats in the old bullring in downtown Tijuana. I felt underdressed in my Levis and T-shirt; many of the local women were decked out in high heels, summer suits, and wide-brimmed hats.

"It isn't about winning or losing!" Carlos was impatient. "That's what I'm trying to tell you. It's not a contest."

"Then what is it?" I asked, impatient myself.

"Well, your gringo writer Ernest Hemingway says it's a Ritual of Death." He sounded sarcastic now.

"What do *you* say it is?" By this time I had learned that it was almost impossible to get a direct answer to a direct question from either Carlos or Jorge. Conversation seemed to move the way traffic moved in Tijuana: in no direction at all, or in all directions at once.

"When the matador comes out, watch how he calls the bull," Carlos said, cryptically. I could tell by the tilt of his head, slightly up and away from me, that there was no use in asking any more questions.

But when the first matador swept into the plaza, sparkling in his suit of lights and brandishing his cape, I couldn't restrain myself.

"What do you mean, 'how he calls the bull'?"

All Carlos said was, "Look."

As I watched, the matador faced the massive beast that was pawing the ground fifteen feet away from him. He seemed to impale the animal with his eyes, fixing him with an intense gaze. The bull stopped pawing and stood motionless, returning the man's gaze. The two remained that way for almost a full minute, locked in a mutual absorption that shocked me with its intimacy. Then the matador gave his cape the slightest flick, never taking his eyes from the eyes of the bull. As if drawn by a secret cord, the bull began to move, running toward the man, head down, horns out. The matador's body was absolutely still, every muscle poised and perfect, like a stag scenting the wind. Only his hands moved, sweeping a sudden circle of cape across his body and leading the bull's head in an arc that passed only inches from his legs. The bull stopped behind the matador, facing away from him, immobile. The crowd roared "*¡Olé!*" and I exhaled the breath I had not known I was holding. My heart was pounding and my palms were wet. Heat and blood and dust filled my nostrils, and I was still shaking when the inevitable moment arrived: The matador raised himself over his bull, long sword poised. I covered my eyes with my hands, peering out from between my fingers. I saw what I knew I would see, what I both feared and needed to see: man and animal, now locked together by a palpable energy, merged into one, joined in the final climactic plunge of the blade into yielding flesh. The bull sank to its knees. The crowd rose up, roaring. I buried my face in Carlos's shoulder and wept.

Our regular visits to Sevillano's had taken on the air of pleasant social calls, and I had almost forgotten about the guitars. As my Spanish improved, I began to listen intently to the conversations during those visits, trying to glimpse the story I believed must lie hidden behind the reserve and the modesty of this remarkable craftsman. I learned only that he had come north years before from a poor village in central Mexico to seek a better life in the bustling commerce of the border. I learned that he closed his shop every Monday to take his wife to the market and that he was an avid fan of the Los Angeles Dodgers, even before the young Fernando Valenzuela came up from Mexico to pitch. It would be years before I knew him well enough to ask him how he had learned his art. Then he would simply shrug and reply, "Everyone in my village makes guitars."

During August's visit the conversation in the shop centered around baseball. The Dodgers were playing the Padres in San Diego the following Sunday, and Jorge and Carlos planned to meet Don Miguel at the stadium along with his two sons, his brother, his brother-in-law, and a few nephews. Suddenly, in the middle of the discussion, Sevillano said, "Ah!" and disappeared into the back room. He emerged with two gleaming guitars, one in each hand, which he handed to Bob and to me without a word. I sat on the Corona carton and ran my hand again and again over the smooth curves of the instrument. I inhaled its warm wood-and-fresh lacquer smell. I strummed a C chord, then a G, then a D. My fingers were trembling, but the sounds they brought forth were full and rich, the strings sensitive and responsive to my touch. The guitar almost played itself; it made me sound better than I was.

"Do you like your little classical, *señora*?" Don Miguel addressed me directly for the first time since we had met. I answered him in Spanish:

"*Sí, Don Miguel, sí, me gusta mucho. Gracias.*" He knelt down beside me and pointed through the strings to the label inside. In black scrolled letters it read "Miguel Sevillano" along with the month and the year.

Bob gave me an E, and we tuned to each other. He sang "Here Comes the Sun" and I followed along. Then we both sang "Peaceful Easy Feelin'," and by that time the boy was back with the beer and Carlos and Jorge had guitars in their hands. When they sang "*De Colores*," my guitar and I sang the harmony. Then they did "*La Bamba*," and my fingers found the beat, and at the chorus I stood up and began to dance, hips loose and easy, moving from the waist.

El Rosario

Ay de mi, Llorona, Llorona
Llorona, llévame al río;
tápame con tu rebozo, Llorona
porque me muero de frío.

Woe is me, *Llorona, Llorona*
Llorona, carry me to the river;
cover me with your shawl, *Llorona,*
for I am dying of cold.

—Mexican folk song, "La Llorona"

After Labor Day the Santa Ana winds began to blow in hot and dry from the desert. Brush fires erupted all over San Diego County like warning flares of doomsday, and smoke billowed across the sun, turning the sky an ominous blood red. My life pressed down with the weight of a storm cloud. My daughter Cathy was in tears every day after school—according to her day-care provider—and she avoided the other children. At home in the evenings she was as sullen as the weather. One night she stubbed her toe coming out of the bathtub and slumped onto the floor in the hallway, crying disconsolately.

"Mommy," she sobbed, "I'm so unhappy!" I knelt on the rug beside her and gathered her into my lap, damp and warm and hiccuping in her towel. I rocked her as I had when she was tiny, and smoothed the limp blond strands that drooped over her brow. The divorce, I thought guiltily. My work, I thought, despairing. As a pediatrician, I was spending hours every day taking care of other people's children; was I neglecting my own? Cathy had invented a new jump-rope chant which I had heard her singing over and over one day in the driveway as she skipped rope all alone. It went: "Two, four, six, eight! Let the patients sit and wait!" The refrain haunted me for weeks, pounding dully in time with my heart.

Joshua seemed to be doing fine in kindergarten, or so I thought until I attended my first parent-teacher conference.

"Josh's academic skills are excellent," said Mrs. Clark. "He's a bright boy."

"How's he doing socially?" I asked apprehensively.

"Well," she said, looking grave, "He had a little problem with one of the girls in the class."

Dear God, I thought, *not already!* I said, "What happened?"

Mrs. Clark's mouth twitched. "It seems Stephanie Larkin has become quite smitten with Josh," she began, "and she asked him if he would marry her. He told her No, and to stop bothering him. So she bit him. On the nose. He's been withdrawn ever since." I laughed until the tears came, tears of relief and regret. Where had I been when my son needed me? Who else would help him understand a scorned woman's fury?

Driving back to work that day, I couldn't concentrate on the road. Images of my children billowed across the windshield, blocking my view: Cathy, my once sunny, golden-haired girl, as sweet and pink as a summer strawberry; funny, loving little Josh with his dark intensity and lightning flashes of joy. All afternoon, in my office at Children's Hospital, their images hovered. Between patients, I figured and refigured budgets. Could I afford to leave the security of my full-time position for a part-time job? By the time I drove home that evening, I had made up my mind. The new roof, the new car would wait. Cathy and Josh wouldn't.

Sue worked as a nurse at a clinic for migrant farm workers and their families, and she suggested I apply there. At my interview, I told the director that I was bilingual. I didn't mention that most of my Spanish came from popular songs, so that I knew how to say "Make this night last forever" but had no idea how to say "Stick out your tongue."

They hired me anyway, as a part-time pediatric consultant. Besides allowing me to be home with the kids after school, the new job provided me with frequent informal Spanish lessons, and I soon learned to say not only "Stick out your tongue," but also "I'm very happy to see you again," "Please give my regards to all your family," and "Thank you for the delicious tamales." The pay was marginal, but I loved the work.

Being home in the afternoons gave me time to practice with my own children what I had always preached to my patients' families. Cathy started seeing a counselor once a week, a friend of mine from Children's Hospital. After dropping her off for her appointment, Josh and I would go to a nearby pond and feed the ducks or catch grasshoppers. Then the three of us would go out for a treat: a meal at McDonald's, or a bargain-time movie with a giant tub of popcorn. By November, we had all begun to feel a little better.

Nonetheless, I was grateful when Bob and Sue invited me to join them for Thanksgiving, especially since it was my ex-husband's turn to have the kids and I dreaded being alone that day. Jorge and Carlos were there, as well as Bob and Sue's eight-year-old daughter Linda, whose dandelion mane matched that of their golden retriever, Leo. After dinner, Carlos and Jorge and Bob and I tuned up the guitars, and we sang for hours, with Sue calling out requests. Finally, after the nineteenth verse of "*La Llorona*," Sue and I went into the kitchen to deal with the dishes.

I was drying the turkey pan when she said, "Bob and Linda and I are going to drive to Mulegé after Christmas. There's room for you and Cathy and Josh if you want to come." From the map of Baja, which I had studied during the trips to Sevillano's, I knew that Mulegé was a town on the Sea of Cortés, about six hundred miles south of the border. "We'll take our time going down there," Sue was saying, "so the kids won't get too restless. There are plenty of places to camp along the way, and we can all share a big room in the old hotel in Mulegé. It won't cost much."

"Sounds fun," I said cautiously.

"Paul could cover your patients for you," she said—referring to one of my colleagues at the clinic. "It would do you good to get away."

"Let me think about it," I told her, calculating income and expenses in my mind.

The Friday after Thanksgiving, I took the kids to the local YMCA to buy a Christmas tree. A twenty-foot-high inflated Santa Claus bobbed in the breeze. "White Christmas" blared over a loudspeaker into the warm southern California afternoon. Cathy found a scrawny tree propped in a corner of the lot.

"Look, Mom," she crooned, "this one looks so sad. It needs a home!"

"That's a dumb tree," said Josh. He had trouble pronouncing the letter *r*, so what he really said was, "That's a dumb twee."

"It is *not* dumb. It's cute!" Cathy put her arms protectively around her tree and promptly broke off one of the brittle branches. From the other end of the lot, the young man in charge looked our way. Quickly, I picked up the closest intact tree and held it up in front of the broken limb.

"I like this one," I said.

"I hate that one," said Josh.

"What about *this* one?" wailed Cathy. The loudspeaker was croaking out "Silver Bells" as I drove away, my Toyota station wagon trailing pine branches, my fingers sticky with pitch.

I was picking the shards of a broken glass ornament from the living room rug when the phone rang. Cathy and Josh were arguing loudly over whose stocking was bigger while on TV a glowing child in his father's arms set a perfect star on the top of a perfect tree. From the kitchen, picking up the receiver, I could see that our tree was listing dangerously to the left. Sue's voice greeted me.

"We're making up the clinic schedule for December," she said. "Are you going to be here the week after Christmas?"

"No," I answered, pulling a strand of tinsel from my hair. "I'm going to Mulegé!"

Even on a map, the peninsula of Baja California appears to occupy its own space, trailing from the body of the North American continent like a phantom limb. And, like a phantom limb, that gnarled appendage maintains a stubborn life of its own, part fantasy and part reality. Politically, the two states of Baja California and Baja California Sur belong to the Republic of Mexico. Historically, the peninsula comprises part of the once-mythic world known in sixteenth-century Spain as *Las Californias* — fabled as the domain of beautiful female warriors, slayers of men and guardians of fabulous treasure: pearls and gold, silver and tourquoise. But in truth, the land of Baja has never belonged to anyone but its own mysterious gods.

Through the centuries, countless adventurers have challenged those gods. In the sixteenth and seventeenth centuries, the Spanish *conquistadores* came seeking riches for their king and for themselves. But even the famed Hernán Cortés, who had brought low the great Aztec empire of Moctezuma and Cuauhtémoc, retreated in frustration from Lower California, thwarted by Indians, by desert, by unpredictable seas—thwarted, in short, by Baja itself, and its implacable gods. By the last decade of the seventeenth century, the Spanish king turned over the colonization of Baja California to the Jesuit priests. The Jesuits, eager to save new souls, agreed to finance their own expeditions in return for permission to explore and settle the land. Thus, in 1697, the first permanent mission was established in California in the town of Loreto, to be followed by a flowering of missions throughout the lower half of the peninsula. Expelled for political reasons in 1768, the Jesuits were followed by the Franciscans and finally by the Dominicans. For a century and a half, the padres traversed the Californias, their missions extending as far north as Sonoma in Upper California (*Alta California*) and as far south as San José del Cabo at the tip of Baja California.

The legacy of the missionary priests was a mixed one. To a people who had, for generations, lived in harmony as hunters and gatherers, they bequeathed agriculture with its labor-intensive demands. For a people who had never seen a window or a door, they built great churches. They preached Christianity to souls who were already intimately connected to their own gods. And ultimately, the padres and their followers brought death in the form of European diseases—syphillis, measles, and smallpox— which all but extinguished Baja's indigenous tribes.

As they traveled through desert and mountain, the padres forged primitive roads connecting their missions and settlements to one another. Boulder by boulder, inch by inch, these trails were wrested from the stubborn land by Indian labor, by the soldiers sent from Spain to guard the holy fathers, and sometimes by the holy fathers themselves. Many of the mission churches have returned to the clay from which they arose, and many of the padres' orchards have long since withered and died. But many of their well-traveled paths remain, and in parts of Upper California their road still bears the name by which it was known three centuries ago: *El Camino Real*, the royal road. It was this same *camino real* which we would follow, in part, on our own journey into Baja California.

December of 1978 turned out to be the wettest month in recent memory in southern California and, as we would find out, in Baja as well. The freeways gridlocked and surface streets flooded. My roof leaked a little, but a couple of buckets to catch the drips prevented any major damage. In truth, being born and bred in Philadelphia, I appreciated the advent of some real weather for a change. The sound of rain on the roof at night and the wood smell of smoke from neighbors' chimneys made it seem more like Christmas. Then, as if to honor the holiday, the sun came out on the twenty-fourth and shimmered over a polished world of crystal leaves and grass. I took it as a good omen, having heard enough tales about the perils of travel in Baja to be thankful for clear skies and dry roads.

We crossed the border just before 9:00 A.M. on the twenty-sixth, and turned onto the toll road to Ensenada which lay seventy miles to the south. We followed the Pacific Ocean along breathtaking cliffs and beaches.

In Ensenada, we pulled into a Pemex station for gas.

"We always fill up here," explained Bob. "You can never be sure where or when you'll find the next gas!"

"The AAA Travel Guide says there's a gas station in San Quintín," I said hopefully.

Bob chuckled. He was a Baja veteran, having driven in his young years down the whole length of the peninsula along the the old road, a boulder-strewn track famed as a maker of men and destroyer of vehicles. Those who had traversed it considered themselves a breed apart. In fact, the paved road had only been completed five years before, in late 1973, and was reputed to be rugged enough for my taste.

"Oh, there's a gas station in San Quintín, all right," Bob observed dryly. "It may or may not have any gas, though."

"What do we do if there's no gas?" I asked, trying to sound nonchalant. I wanted to impart a sense of fun and adventure to my kids, who were blithely playing jacks with Linda on the floor of the van.

"If there's no gas, we just hang out until the gas truck shows up," said Bob, starting the engine. "This is Baja."

South of Ensenada the countryside opens up into a wide, fertile plain. In a dry land any water is precious, and the farming community of Maneadero clings to a seasonal stream that irrigates its fields and washes away its roads in times of rain. We churned through mud for miles, once making a cross-country detour where the mud looked too deep even for a Volkswagen van. The kids squealed with delight at each bounce and swerve, and Sue and Bob seemed completely unperturbed. Peace flowed from the earth in waves of green and brown and drifted through the windows of the van. I began to relax.

We climbed a range of low mountains and descended into a narrow canyon where yellow sycamores shimmered by a stream and the sun glinted off the Pacific Ocean beyond rolling hills to the west. Then we chugged slowly up a long, steep grade around heart-stopping blind curves whose victims were numbered by the small shrines lining the roadside. At last, with a grateful sigh, we rolled down into the gentle valley of Santo Tomás. In that welcoming land the Dominican padres, two centuries before, had planted their vineyards, reminders of home. Their grapevines still shone gold in the December sun as we descended.

"Who's hungry?" called Sue, and soon we were sitting on my old quilt under a pepper tree eating Christmas turkey sandwiches from home while a herd of goats ambled by, bells clanking softly. The weathered old goatherd pushed his cowboy hat off his eyebrows and flashed us his gums as he passed.

"*Que les vaya bien,*" he murmured, "May it go well with you." Beside me three small heads—sand, honey, mahogany—bent intently over a red beetle. Before me blue cloud shadows slid lazily over green velvet mountains. Somewhere behind me, three hours to the north, cars sped endlessly from freeway to freeway in a race with no finish line, no winners.

"We'll be through El Rosario by 3:00." Sue leaned back on her elbows and watched clouds drift as she spoke. "We can camp in the desert at Cataviña tonight."

All three children were asleep on the back seat, leaning into one another, when we saw the volcanoes. San Quintín Bay is a vast, shallow harbor—usually windy, often adrift in fog. Far to one end of the bay, three volcanic cones rise against the sky like sentinels guarding an ungentle land. Their prehistoric silhouettes were the first sight to greet the band of English colonists who settled in San Quintín in the late 1800s at the invitation of the Mexican government. Under the indifferent shadow of the volcanoes, those hopeful newcomers planted English wheat, built a mill for grinding, and a pier for shipping their crops. But after a few dry seasons most of the colonists lay under little wooden crosses on a windswept marsh. The few who survived sailed back to the green fields of England, leaving behind forever the unforgiving gods of Baja.

Many years later, on a moonless night of heavy fog, those gods would guide Carlos and me to safe haven in San Quintín, when all we had in the whole black world to steer by were the volcanoes, their dark, familiar forms looming like old friends above the fog bank.

"Pemex ahoy!" yelled Bob. He swung the van off the road and into the most chaotic gas-station line I had ever seen. We all got out, stretching, the kids rubbing their eyes sleepily. There were at least a dozen vehicles waiting for one gas pump, and they were crowding onto the little Pemex island from all directions. The two attendants manning the pump gave no sign of hurry or pressure. Indeed, the crowd milling around, mostly vacationing Americans, had a mellow air. Everyone seemed to be taking the delay in stride: just another Baja adventure. Rumors, however, flew like tumbleweed in a sandstorm.

"I heard there's no more gas between here and Guerrero Negro."

"No gas in Cataviña?"

"Well, there wasn't any yesterday when I drove through. They were expecting the truck today or tomorrow."

"Looks like they might run out here, too."

I was gazing out at the flat, dry country, picturing ancient gatherings around ancient oases in other desert lands. Suddenly I heard someone say, "The road south of El Rosario is gone." Bob had been leaning against the van, arms folded across his chest, eyes closed, face tilted to the sun. Now he opened his eyes and removed the toothpick from the corner of his mouth.

"The road's out?" he asked the man who had spoken.

"Yeah," answered the man who, on closer inspection, looked more like a college kid. "We got through on Christmas Eve, barely. By yesterday morning, *adiós* road!" He waved gaily, pushing back his Giants cap from his forehead.

"I guess our rain moved south, hit here yesterday," said Bob to Sue who had herded the children together and had come over to hear the news.

"Well," Sue said firmly, "I'm certainly not going back. Anyone want to go back?"

"Nooo!" shouted the kids in unison. "Noo!" I echoed, laughing.

"OK by me," said Bob. "We go on, road or no road."

"The Adventure Club," cried Sue, and held out her hand, palm up. "The Six Musketeers," yelled Linda, slapping her mother's palm. Cathy did a little prance and Josh called out, "All wight!" And standing there on the grimy concrete of the Pemex station in San Quintín, we made a slapping, giggling pile of six hands. Then I put an arm around each of my children, and pulled Linda in beside Cathy. "Let's go to the beach," I suggested. "We're going to be here awhile."

An hour later, damp and loaded with sand dollars, we climbed back into the van and headed south with a tank full of gas. The road deteriorated badly, and Bob had to drive in wide arcs to avoid wheel-crunching potholes. In several spots, the road disappeared; the tire tracks of our predecessors were the only signs to the dirt detours. It was almost 5:00 and the sun was low in the sky when we finally drove into the little hamlet of El Rosario.

In the days before the paved road, when any foray into Baja was an exercise in survival, El Rosario was the last outpost of civilization before the old road turned inland to cross more than two hundred miles of treacherous desert. For many years Anita Espinosa had run the small café and store that still marked the entrance to town. She was famous among Baja buffs for her unfailing hospitality to road-weary travelers and her unfailing knowledge of road conditions. In fact, she was one of a series of legendary *doñas* of Baja, tough angels who ministered to pilgrims found wandering in that wilderness: Doña Josefina of Cataviña, Doña Blanca of Loreto, Mama Díaz of Bahía de los Angeles.

Beyond Doña Anita's establishment a dirt road curved to the west.

A flock of seagulls wheeled in a cobalt sky over the gold furrows of plowed fields; a handful of little houses in pastel shades dotted the unpaved road. To the east, the paved highway ran bravely on for a half mile and then disappeared completely into a hundred-yard-wide gully of muddy water where the river churned through to the sea. Chunks of highway bobbed upon the flood like so many fisherman's floats. We came to a stop at the end of a line of five or six cars parked on the road just west of the gully. On the east side, vehicles stretched away for a quarter of a mile, most of them parked off the road, many with tents sprouting beside them like mushrooms.

A young man was wading across the river toward town, waist deep in muck, holding aloft two plastic gallon jugs for drinking water, both empty. I ran through a rapid mental checklist, switching automatically into survival mode: water, food, shelter. Cathy's stuffed Snoopy, Josh's old blue blanket. Check.

Bob had fallen silent, staring morosely through the windshield at the cold mud. Sue had shifted into her take-charge mode. The three children were sorting sand dollars on the van floor, piling them up by size.

"OK," said Sue, "we have one tent and the van. Three and three: me and Bob and Linda in the tent, Judy and her kids in the van."

"Where do you think we should camp?" I asked. The fields on the west side of the road were lower than those on the east and looked soggy.

"Up where the houses are it's a little higher and dryer," Bob said. He turned and looked back over his shoulder to the town. "Let's see if we can find someone's front lawn. Maybe we can rent ourselves a campsite."

The Duartes lived in a bubblegum pink house set back from the dirt road by a dirt yard where magenta geraniums sprouted in tin washtubs and an old camper shell rusted away among tires and engine parts. Behind the house, red chiles dried on every possible surface: they spread over the ground and over the roof of the hen house, they hung from the walls, and they even shared the clothesline with Señor Duarte's overalls. Only the twin outhouses, at the far end of the property, were spared.

Señora Duarte opened the door immediately when we knocked, as if she had been expecting us. Her husband stood behind her, and four pairs of small round eyes peered out from behind him until a woman's voice called sharply from the dim interior. The elder Duartes were both tall and stooped and gray, and their bodies were bent in the same direction, as if they had been blown for many years by the same wind. They regarded us calmly, unsurprised to find six *norteamericanos* on their doorstep seeking shelter. Pitch a tent in their yard? Certainly not; we were not gypsies! But their home was our home. There were two beds, they pointed out, one for each family. Where would they sleep? we asked. This question was dismissed with a wave of the hand as too trivial to even answer. We were ushered in and shown two tiny bedrooms, each just large enough for the one double bed it contained. The beds were still rumpled from their previous night's occupants and looked comfortable, like home. Night and the temperature were both falling fast, and we accepted their offer gratefully, with no further discussion. I was too tired and bewildered at the time to reflect on the Duartes' unconditional hospitality. But months later, remembering that night, I wondered how I would have reacted to six bedraggled strangers on my doorstep at twilight asking in broken English to camp on my front lawn.

The turkey sandwiches had long since worn off, and the children were beginning to droop and whine with hunger. Sue and I dug out cans of soup and boxes of crackers from the van, while Bob, encouraged by Señor Duarte's assurance that the road would be repaired tomorrow, checked tires and oil. Señora Duarte lit a kerosene lamp on her kitchen table, and I poured soup into a battered pot on her stove, adding water from a clay jug she offered. Beside the stove, the kitchen opened onto a wooden porch. Just beyond the porch, the dirt road stretched out past the candy-colored houses toward the sea.

An ancient black Chevrolet, radio and muffler both blaring, drove back and forth, back and forth along the road, pursued by two dogs yelping joyfully. The young driver of the car had strung colored lights to his windshield, and they flashed in sequence, round and round. The Chevy's brash gaiety was the only sign of Christmas in the village.

Señora Duarte nodded and smiled as the three children devoured the soup. Her own extensive family had disappeared into the night, and soon she, too, slipped away with a quiet "*Buenas noches.*"

It was surprisingly warm with the three of us in bed together, despite the cold air and thin covers. Cathy settled against me as gently as the sea mist settling outside, and Josh's tough little limbs wound around mine and clung. I lay awake for a long time, holding them both close and inhaling their smells, sweat and earth and vegetable-beef soup. El Rosario's lone cruiser had finally gone home, and there was no sound but my children's regular breathing. Sleep, when it came, was deep and dreamless.

In the morning Sue and Bob made coffee on our camp stove while the kids, guided by giggling Duarte grandchildren, collected fresh eggs from the hen house. I pulled a clean sweatshirt out of my bag in the van and walked down the road toward the gully, straining my eyes for a glimpse of a bulldozer or at least a few men with shovels. All I saw was the same line of cars as the previous night and a good many rumpled gringos slouched by the roadside.

"Any sign of the bulldozer?"

"They said the governor was sending two of 'em down here yesterday!"

"Town's runnin' out of food and water."

"Gal on the other side needs insulin. Can't get it here."

Panic was gathering, spreading its ugly tentacles. I thought I felt its icy touch on my own throat, and turned back quickly to the little pink house on the hill floating like a rosy balloon in the morning sun. As I approached, I saw Señor and Señora Duarte on the porch with Bob and Sue. The three children had been engulfed by a herd of local kids that swarmed the front yard, taking turns pulling one another around in a cardboard box. Bob handed me a cup of coffee, and I leaned against the wooden rail.

"No one seems to be working on the road," I remarked, in Spanish.

Señor Duarte smiled and nodded indulgently, just as Señora Duarte had smiled and nodded at the hungry children the previous night. "*Mañana*" was all he said.

Sue poured another round of coffee. "How many children do you have?" she asked our hosts.

Señora Duarte rocked a little in her chair. "Eight living," she answered, "and two that have died."

"And how many grandchildren?" I asked, remembering the round eyes that had peered at us from inside the house.

Both Duartes laughed. "*Muchos*," replied Señora Duarte. "*Demasiados*," smiled Señor Duarte, shaking his head. "Too many!"

"Does all your family live here in El Rosario?" I was thinking that they must comprise the entire town.

"All here except Juan. He has gone to the other side."

"*El otro lado?*" I repeated the Spanish phrase, puzzled. I thought perhaps Juan was one of the ones who had died. Did she mean that he had gone to Heaven and the other had not? Was this some arcane folk belief?

"Yes," she was saying, "but he sends us money when he can, and he comes home sometimes for a month or two."

I frowned my confusion at Bob.

"'*El otro lado*' means the United States," he explained. "Their son Juan must be working in the States."

I considered the phrase in my mind. "He has gone to the other side." It suggested a place so distant, so extraordinary, that no proper noun would suffice. It suggested an altered state of existence. I looked at the Duartes, weathering quietly in the morning sun along with the wood of the porch they had built. I watched their uncountable progeny tumble forth to populate the town. I gazed down the road to where the river reclaimed its ancient course, heedless of stranded tourists. Far on the other side, the peninsula stretched away in the mist *hacía el otro lado*.

We woke the following morning to the distant chug of an engine. A bulldozer was pushing mud around the gully, but it would be another day before the road was passable. In the meantime, Bob spent hours with Señor Duarte in his olive grove across from the house. Under the shade of the silver trees the two ranchers spoke of water and weather, sowing and reaping. Four years later we would pay our last respects to Señor Duarte where he lay at rest beneath those same trees, to be joined, in due time, by his *señora*.

While the men swapped ranch talk, Sue and I accompanied Señora Duarte among her chiles and chickens, and sat with her on the porch while an endless tide of children, ours among them, surged about our feet.

On the second morning of our stay, two skinny boys, whom we had not seen before, approached us carrying a nylon shopping bag that appeared to be writhing. "The mayor sends you these lobsters," said the taller boy, "and invites you to his home this evening." Sue and I looked at each other and then into the bag. Eight antennae waved back at us. "Please tell the mayor that we are very grateful to him," said Sue in Spanish. "It would please us very much to visit him this evening."

Señora Duarte, who had been sitting on the porch with us, went into the kitchen and emerged with a large pot. Closing my eyes and calling upon the spirits of all the *doñas* of Baja, I grabbed two of the spiny creatures and dropped them into the pot. Sue got the other two, and we returned the bag to the boys who called "*¡Hasta luego!*" as they ran off. We agreed that, having been honored by such a gift, we should share it with the Duartes; to make the lobster stretch, we decided to prepare a New England style stew for the afternoon meal. Cathy and Josh were peering into the pot in horrified fascination. Linda, farm girl and daughter of the seacoast, skipped with delight. "I love lobster!" she crowed.

"Are we going to *eat* those things?" Cathy gasped.

"I hate lobstuh!" announced Josh.

To spare them, I sent Cathy and Josh to the van for milk and butter from the cooler while we boiled the still-squirming animals. Linda chopped carrots and potatoes, unperturbed. Bob came up with Señor Duarte from the fields, and soon the six of us were digging meat out of shells while lobster juice ran down our arms and onto the cement floor. The Duartes looked on dubiously. Lobsters were almost as common as chiles in El Rosario, but were eaten boiled or grilled over mesquite wood, never simmered in milk. At 1:30 that afternoon, I ladled out the first bowl of stew to the *señora*, who lifted a gray eyebrow and nodded her approval when she tasted it.

By 2:00, there were people all over the kitchen, on the porch, on the stairs to the porch, and sitting on inverted washtubs in the yard— all eating lobster stew from bowls, cups, glasses, and saucepans; and still they came, from every direction, all of El Rosario bearing spoons and receptacles, and all hungry. Beside me, Josh held out his bowl for a third helping. Strands of pink meat dangled from his chin. His mouth was still full as he declared, "I love lobstuh!"

The miraculous stew finally disappeared. After washing the pot (searching it for clues to the magic that had fed the whole town on four lobsters), we joined the rest of El Rosario in a siesta. Around 5:00 we arose and dressed in the cleanest clothes we had; I made the children scrub their faces with the cold well-water in the back yard, which was used for washing. At last, guided by one of the Duartes' sons and escorted by cacophonous dogs, we filed down the dirt road to a mint-green house near the abalone packing plant at the end of town. The mayor himself opened the door. He was a hearty, corpulent man of about forty with a balding head and thick black mustache. In the living room, two other men were sitting on a plastic-covered red brocade sofa. Above them on the wall hung a photograph of JFK in a scrolled frame, dimly visible in the light from a kerosene lamp on the coffee table. The only other piece of furniture in the room was a large TV in an elaborately carved wood console that sat in the middle of the floor, its electric cord neatly coiled beside it. As far as I knew, the nearest source of electric power was in Ensenada, more than two hundred miles away.

The other men rose as we entered, and we all shook hands, exchanging names. Bob sat on the sofa, and chairs were brought in from another room for Sue and me. The children sat on our laps.

"*¿Tequilita?*" The mayor was addressing Bob as he lifted an open bottle of Cuervo Gold from the coffee table; his *compadres* were already drinking. Bob and the mayor toasted to each other's health and downed their shooters. "Would the *señoras* care for a cocktail?" The mayor addressed the question to Bob. Bob eyed us with mock gravity, feigning proprietorship. I pictured a cold, frothy margarita and tried not to salivate.

"Yes," answered Bob, "I believe the *señoras* would enjoy a cocktail." The mayor shouted something in the direction of the kitchen, and a slender young woman—whom I took to be his wife—appeared with a tray. She bowed slightly toward Sue and me, and handed us each a parfait glass filled with chopped abalone, cilantro, onion, and hot sauce. *¡Cocteles de mariscos!* Of course, I thought, I should have known: tequila cocktails for the men, seafood cocktails for the ladies. They tasted delicious, but Sue and I couldn't look at each other as we ate them, eyes watering from the chiles and from our suppressed giggles.

For the next hour Bob fielded a barrage of questions about life *en el otro lado*: How much did we pay for a loaf of bread? Was it really true that everyone drove a new car? Did we know Las Vegas? Chivalrously ignored, Sue and I chatted quietly while the kids played with a skinny tabby cat who seemed to appreciate the attention.

As we were taking our leave, I asked the mayor the question I had been carefully preparing in Spanish. "*Señor Alcalde*," I said, shaking his hand, "your television is beautiful. But is it not true that there is no electricity here?"

The mayor smiled, showing perfect teeth. "*Ah, señora*," he answered, "one day electricity will come to El Rosario. Maybe next year, maybe in five years. But when it comes, I will be the first in town to turn on a TV."

The mist had not yet rolled in as we walked back; the night was clear and cold. Far above us, arpeggios of stars chimed in a deep black sky. A rectangle of amber light marked the Duartes' doorway, and their silhouettes leaned against the door frame, waiting. For a moment I felt like a teenager coming home to find Mom and Dad watching for me. I was flooded with a sense of security and protection that I had almost forgotten.

"The road is ready," announced Señor Duarte. "You must leave early, before it sinks again."

Cuddled in our bed that night, I told Cathy and Josh, "This little pink house has been a good home-away-from-home for us. Let's always remember it." Cathy said, sleepily, "I thought you said the van was our home-away-from-home." Josh murmured, "home- away-from-home-away-from-home."

"Go to sleep, *mis niños*," I said, gathering them to me.

Mulegé

. . . color del cielo,	. . . the color of the sky,
color del mar . . .	the color of the sea . . .
Azul como una ojera de mujer	Blue like the shadow of a woman's eyes
como un listón, azul	Blue like a ribbon,
azul de amanecer.	Like the blue of dawn.

—Augustín Lara, "Azul"

When the intrepid padres forged the old *camino real*, bringing Christianity and near-extinction to the natives of Baja, they followed ancient Indian trails that led from water to water. In places, the road still traces their footsteps, zig-zagging through the arid land along the shortest course from river to spring to well. Studying the AAA map, I could see that the three hundred miles we had covered between Tijuana and El Rosario included ten thin blue lines meriting the name *río*. South of El Rosario, however, there stretched almost three hundred miles of empty tan-and-white map before the word *río* appeared again over a thin blue line. In fact, it was the first road map I had ever seen on which wells and springs were marked as prominently as towns. By my count, there were two wells, three springs, and one little blue square labeled *Agua Amarga* (Bitter Water) between us and that far away *río* to the south. Reflexively, I looked up from the map and glanced to the back of the van, confirming that our five-gallon bottles of water were still there.

The day had started auspiciously. By 7:00 in the morning we were in line behind a Dodge pickup truck, waiting for our turn to cross the river. The road repair had simply consisted of piling dirt into the riverbed until it was high enough to traverse. Overnight, of course, the dirt had turned to slick mud; I understood what Mr. Duarte had meant when he cautioned us to cross early, "before it sinks again." It was clearly a one-lane affair, and the little group of stranded travelers had developed into a kind of community, cheering each other on as, one by one, vehicles bounced and skidded and careened across the gully. Sue was at the wheel of the van, Bob having spent a miserable night in the outhouse—a victim of too much Cuervo Gold. I rode shotgun, road map spread on my lap.

When our turn came to navigate the muddy crossing, all three kids pressed eagerly against the front seats, anticipating an adventure. Sue sat up very straight in the driver's seat and gripped the steering wheel squarely at ten and two o'clock. A little crowd on the east side of the gully shouted encouragement.

"Hold on!" cried Sue, and she hit the gas, guiding the bucking van into the tire tracks of the Dodge. The three children shrieked with delight, and I heard myself yell "Yahoo!" as we climbed onto the pavement and turned south. In the back seat Bob groaned. We were on the road again.

The morning sky was still streaked with gold and crimson over the mountains to our left as we headed southeast toward the next spring of water, seventy-five miles and over two hours away. The road was like swiss cheese, with deep holes everywhere, and the driving was tortuous. Bob slumped against a window in the back seat, eyes closed, but the rest of us watched the landscape unfold with a growing sense of enchantment.

The desert stretched in all directions, silent and still. It was like no desert I had ever imagined. Squadrons of *cardón* cactus marched to the horizon, raising their massive arms fifteen feet or more into the brightening sky. Boojum trees, gangly and graceful, curled their limbs into weird arabesques, or extended them upward like the branches of a candelabrum; the Spanish padres had named them *cirios* after the tall candelabra that lit the mission churches. Between the *cirios* sprawled the low and deceptively lovely chollas, sometimes called "devil cactus" for their treacherous thorns that now glowed like little halos, backlit by the morning sun. To my right, out of the desert stillness, a hawk climbed in a high spiral, his red tail shining in the rising light. A crow glared at us from his perch atop an ancient *cardón*.

It was as though our small van were a spaceship or a bathysphere, carrying us through a world never meant for humankind. Here and there, weathered signs announced valiant bids for human survival: *Rancho El Progreso*, where the sign itself was the only evidence of man's presence; *Rancho Arenoso*, sandy as its name, where one thin cow, grazing dry chaparral, was the sole representative of mammalian life.

By 8:30 the kids were beginning to whine and squabble, a sure sign of hunger. I was nursing a caffeine-withdrawal headache; in our anxiety to leave El Rosario early and get across the river, we had skipped coffee and breakfast. Fifteen miles ahead lay Cataviña, a small oasis fed by freshwater springs where the Mexican government had recently established a Pemex station and hotel, and where Rancho Santa Inés, one of Baja's oldest working ranches, had long welcomed travelers with food and lodging. The ranch was owned by the legendary Doña Josefina, famous for her enchiladas, her hospitality, and—according to some sources—her supernatural powers. We agreed to take a break when we got there, fueling the van and ourselves.

Although I had grown up thousands of miles from any desert and had never before been in one, the sudden sight of blue palm trees rising from limpid pools amid giant white boulders brought a lump of nostalgia to my throat, as if I were coming home. Perhaps we all carry an inbred genetic survival mechanism, programmed to respond emotionally to water in a desert place. Perhaps, as some have claimed, Cataviña is a spot of special energy, a vortex of power. Or perhaps I was just hungry and caffeine-starved. The clean fragrance of sage floated through the open window, and the very air seemed to vibrate: Finches undulated from mesquite to mesquite, weaving a web of song; springs bubbled by the road and splashed across the blacktop; palm leaves rustled above enormous boulders of granite. While Bob, who had rallied, gassed up at the Pemex station, Sue and the children and I took off our shoes and dug our toes into the still-cool sand of the desert. We left our happy footprints on the floor of the van when we climbed back in and, leaving the highway, followed a graded dirt road east toward Rancho Santa Inés and breakfast.

The ranch looked like a picture-book version of a Mexican hacienda. A low whitewashed adobe structure wrapped around three sides of a sandy-floored courtyard, where a long wooden table spread out in the shade of an old palo verde tree. Bougainvillea blossoms exploded purple and orange against the white walls, curling up to the overhanging red roof tiles. A hummingbird buzzed from vine to vine. The left wing of the structure was the kitchen; the wall facing the courtyard was open halfway down, revealing a four-burner propane stove and a stack of steaming tortillas. A young man's face appeared in the opening, his battered felt-hat shading his eyes.

"*Buenos días,*" he called. I could smell coffee, and thought I might swoon right there under the palo verde tree.

"*Buenos días,*" returned Bob. "*¿Hay café?*"

Indeed, there was coffee—strong and laced with cinnamon—fresh flour tortillas, and *machaca con huevos*: dried beef mixed with scrambled eggs and chile. Maybe it was the freshness of all the ingredients or the desert air or simply hunger, but the six of us consumed almost two dozen tortillas and probably as many eggs. By the time we were satiated, the sun was high and warm in the sky, and I was tempted to stretch out in the shade for a siesta. Linda had wandered off to pet a small bay mare tethered to a mesquite tree by a corral. Cathy and Josh had befriended two little ranch dogs, both of whom appeared to be part coyote. Sue and Bob and I were counting out our pesos to the cook and preparing to leave, but I still hadn't caught sight of Doña Josefina and couldn't restrain my curiosity. I had secretly been counting on meeting her.

After my marriage had started to unravel, I had explored the remedies of the day: counseling, support groups, self-help books. But they left me vaguely unsatisfied and still struggling with inchoate, unanswered questions. After my first forays into Tijuana, those questions only multiplied. My friend Marge introduced me to astrology, which seemed to me to be about as helpful as psychology had been, only a lot cheaper. Of course my sister in Philadelphia thought I had finally succumbed completely to the madness of California; perhaps she was right. Nonetheless, I moved from astrology to the books of Carlos Castañeda—harboring a clandestine wish to find my ally in the spirit world, or at least a human guide. Marge had hinted that Doña Josefina was a real *bruja* who might have a message for me. I had never met a real witch before, and I pictured a leathery crone, stooped and toothless under the folds of a black *rebozo*.

In my best Spanish, I asked the young ranch hand, "*¿No se encuentra Doña Josefina?*"

"*No, señora,*" he replied. "*Doña Josefina se fue a San Diego.*"

"San Diego?" I didn't think of witches as traveling to San Diego, and I must have looked surprised, because the young man smiled broadly.

"Yes," he continued in Spanish, "she has property in San Diego. Condominiums, I think."

Some bruja! I thought, disgruntled. What kind of sorceress has condominiums in San Diego? But as we rolled away from the little oasis into the vast, formidable desert beyond, I had to smile to myself. Only a woman of powerful magic would manage not only to survive but also to prosper in this daunting land.

From Cataviña, the road heads south for fifty more miles of enchanted high desert, through forests of *cardón* and *cirio* and the curious elephant tree, whose squat gray trunk and branches appear lifeless during long dry seasons but burst into riotous peach pink blossoms at the first drop of rain. Then the road turns southwest and descends almost two thousand feet into the bleak and windswept Vizcaíno Desert. Bob and the children were asleep in a heap in the backseat, and I was doing my best to keep Sue alert by reading aloud from the AAA guidebook.

"This is one of the most desolate portions of the entire peninsula," I droned. "Extra caution is required in this section, which is characterized by steep drop-offs, sharp curves, and a narrow roadway."

"My God!" cried Sue. "What's that?"

"What?" I dropped the guidebook to the floor as we came around a sharp curve of narrow roadway and headed down a steep drop-off.

"There's a wreck ahead. I see body parts on the road."

Several hundred yards ahead, two decrepit pickup trucks—their beds loaded Baja-style to three times the height of the cab—had apparently collided head-on and were now blocking both lanes. The road was strewn with flesh. I could feel the adrenaline surge as it used to do when I was a young resident on call in the emergency room, and I ran through a quick mental review of CPR procedures, my pulse racing. Bob and the children sat up groggily as Sue brought the van to a stop.

"Distract the children!" she called to Bob, as she and I jumped out. "There's a terrible accident ahead."

It was clear that no amount of CPR was going to help the bits of flesh on the blacktop. I hurried to the roadside looking for whole bodies with signs of life. What I saw were five men running through the desert in all directions, moving in crazy patterns, back and forth and in circles, flapping their arms and yelping unintelligible noises. The hair rose on the back of my neck, and I started thinking about *brujas* again. Then a familiar sound began to sink into my reeling brain: *cluck-cluck-cluck-cluck-cluck*. Chickens were everywhere: squawking across the desert in blind panic, darting recklessly around cactus, and weaving through the chaparral. In hot pursuit were five sweating men cursing loudly in Spanish. The body parts we had seen strewn across the road were drumsticks and wings, and the truck facing south was covered in white feathers. One of the escapees scuttled between Sue's legs, and she snagged it, holding it aloft and calling out to the men.

"Muchas gracias, señora." The trucker who approached Sue to thank her was heavy-set and obviously winded from chasing errant poultry. His red shirt was dark with sweat and his boots were gray with desert dust. The chicken truck turned out to be drivable, although the force of the collision had knocked out a few of the two-by-fours that penned its live cargo. After replacing Sue's captive in its makeshift coop, the driver pulled his feathered vehicle off the road so that we could pass. Bob took the wheel; Sue and I collapsed in slightly hysterical laughter and celebrated the Great Chicken Caper with a cold beer from the cooler. The kids each had a soda, and Bob contented himself with long swigs of water.

For the next hour, the only signs of civilization were an empty Pemex station at Punta Prieta ("No gas there," observed Bob, dryly) and a weather-beaten roadside café optimistically called *La Nueva Esperanza*. But the New Hope restaurant looked hopelessly abandoned, and it wasn't until we reached the government hotel two miles outside of Guerrero Negro that we saw any real evidence of human habitation. We had come almost one hundred fifty miles from the charms of Cataviña. It was 2:00 in the afternoon by my watch, but the eastward slant of the peninsula had carried us into another time zone, and as we crossed the twenty-eighth parallel into Baja California Sur it was suddenly 3:00 and time for lunch. The rough frontier town we entered, despite its romantic name of Black Warrior, looked flat and bleak and charmless. No trees softened its dusty streets, no flowers bloomed around its faded wooden buildings. To our right, a vast marshy plain stretched away for fifteen miles toward the Pacific Ocean and Scammon's Lagoon, where the great gray whales come to give birth and to nurture their young for the long journey back to Alaska. We had originally thought of spending one night at Scammon's, but our unplanned stay in El Rosario had eaten up our whale-watching time. The wild marshland rolled by, punctuated only by basins of dry white salt where sea water had evaporated. Nothing along the road tempted us to stop; we nibbled on cheese and crackers in the van while we filled the tank with gas, following Baja's rule of never passing up a chance to get fuel.

After Guerrero Negro the road headed southeast through mile after monotonous mile of desolation. At first we chattered cheerfully, assuring each other that the next ocean we came to would be the fabled Sea of Cortés. After about thirty minutes we fell silent, dulled by the endless emptiness of the Vizcaíno Desert. By 4:00 P.M. the sun was flinging long umber rays over the chaparral, and the temperature was beginning to sink, along with our spirits. According to the map, the old mission town of San Ignacio lay about forty miles ahead; the thin blue line pointing at the town like an arrow from the west was *Río San Ignacio. ¡Río!* We all needed an oasis, and agreed unanimously to spend the night in San Ignacio.

"I'm bushed," Sue told Bob. "Let's stay at the Hotel Presidente. I could use a hot shower and a clean bed."

"No way!" Bob sounded bushed, too, and irritable. "That place is a giant rip-off. We'll stay at the Posada."

They bickered their way into an angry silence. I cast a mental vote for a hot shower and a clean bed, not knowing anything about either hotel, although my guidebook made it clear that there were only these two choices. By now, mountains had begun to appear to the east, their canyons etched with deep shadows and their rocky slopes with heavy gold light. A curtain of silence had descended on our little group. Even the children had ceased their usual buzz and hum. I hadn't realized how their bright little background song had anchored me; without it, I felt suddenly alone and insubstantial, as if, with the slightest breeze, I would simply drift out the window and disappear into the endless emptiness of land and sky. From a great distance, words from a Robert Frost poem floated into my mind:

> *They cannot scare me with their empty spaces*
> *Between stars—on stars void of human races.*
> *I have it in me so much nearer home*
> *To scare myself with my own desert places.*

It was only an impression of movement, nothing solid; but as I raised my head, I saw him bound across the road, all rippling muscle: lord of cactus and sand, a magnificent coyote, trailing beauty behind him. Just before he vanished in the desert shadows, he turned his head and looked at me. It was then that I saw, on the distant horizon before us, a sudden glint of brightness. As we drove on, the brightness spread and then blossomed into the unmistakable shimmer of water lit by the lowering sun. Palm trees appeared, their cool green color sweet to the eye. Soon we could make out the thatched roofs of houses and the rich blood-red of bougainvillea. We rolled onto a graded dirt road that passed under an arch of date palms and over a river flowing away toward the western sun, deep and tranquil, redolent of wet vegetation. High overhead a crow called once, then circled and flew with great, slow strokes, directly before us. We entered into the town plaza of San Ignacio and parked under a laurel tree across from the old stone mission. Somewhere a radio was playing a song full of sobbing guitars, and for the space of a heartbeat, as I descended onto the cobblestones, I thought I heard Carlos's laugh. But it turned out to be only a youth, joking with a group of friends on the street corner. Two small hands tugged at my elbows, and looking down I saw two small faces peering up at me.

"¿*Dátiles, señora?*" Both children carried baskets of fat, juicy dates. I bought a bag full of fruit from each of them, then herded our kids across the street to a small café, leaving Bob and Sue by the van to debate the relative merits of the town's two hotels.

In the end, they reached a compromise that satisfied no one: We all shared one room at the Presidente (a government owned chain later sold to the La Pinta chain.) The hot water turned out to be barely tepid, and the toilet had plugged up by morning. We overpaid in the restaurant for an almost inedible dinner, and by the time we checked out early the next day, everyone was grumbling.

Before hitting the road for the last push to Mulegé, we stopped at the little café on the plaza for coffee and rolls. While the children fed crumbs to pigeons on the sidewalk and Bob and Sue stared stonily in opposite directions, I contemplated the San Ignacio morning. Sunlight filtered through the broad leafy trees ringing the plaza, and old men settled on shady benches to play dominos or to gossip. The same two children who had sold me their dates were playing on the steps of a central gazebo, joined by three or four other youngsters of various ages. Women strolled by carrying small morning purchases in string bags: one with a package of steaming tortillas, another with a few brown eggs. The mission walls reflected a warm gold light across the plaza and into all the narrow streets of the town. As we paid the young waiter for our breakfast, I told him in Spanish, "I will return some day to San Ignacio."

"*Dios quiera*," he responded. "God willing." Watching the green river and stately palms recede behind us, I sent a silent, fervent prayer to the gods of Baja to bring me back one day to that gentle oasis.

For the next hour we drove through more cactus and chaparral, heading east. To our left, blazing with morning light, rose the barren volcanic cones called The Three Virgins. Once, at the crest of a long rise in the road, we caught sight of the Sea of Cortés shining like a blue and gold mirage before it disappeared again behind a stony hill. At length, we came to the edge of the desert and began a long, winding descent down what the AAA guidebook calls "the steepest grade on the entire length of Highway 1" and Erle Stanley Gardner called "the road of death." Linda and Josh leaned their heads out the window, laughing at the sharp switchbacks as if they were part of a Disneyland ride. Cathy, who was carsick, laid her head on my lap in the backseat. I closed my eyes and tried to breathe deeply.

When the van finally leveled out and I opened my eyes again, I saw dazzling white sand edging a sea of emerald and aquamarine. Everyone started talking at once; even Bob and Sue forgot their feud in the intoxicating ocean air. The kids clamored to get out and go to the beach, but we bribed them with sweet rolls left over from breakfast. Mulegé was only an hour away.

It was a little before noon when, trailing a plume of dust, we bumped over the narrow dirt road into town. A faded yellow grocery store sported a hand-lettered sign that said, *HIELO*.

"Look!" cried Cathy, "How sweet! They're trying to say Hello to us." I didn't have the heart to tell her that *hielo* meant ice. In fact, she was right in spirit: The sign had an unquestionably welcoming air. On the other side of the road, equally welcoming, palm trees bordered the lush banks of the Mulegé River.

The Vieja Hacienda hotel was just that: an old hacienda that had been converted to a hotel when the town grew up around it. Pale green paint peeled from its façade, and the iron gate leading from the street to the interior courtyard creaked on rusty hinges. The courtyard itself looked more like someone's home than like the grounds of a hotel. Old wooden chairs and tables in various stages of decay were scattered haphazardly in the shade of eaves and in the bright sunshine that illuminated the courtyard's center. Bougainvillea and hibiscus sprawled in tangled profusion, untamed by gardener's shears; and between the luxuriant vines, sprouted clumps of wild basil.

Our room opened onto the courtyard, and the high ceiling was crisscrossed with heavy wooden beams. The two double beds sagged, but what they lacked in comfort they had in character, facing a wall-sized fireplace with a stack of firewood beside it. Sue pulled a bright pink-and-orange scarf from her suitcase and draped it over a nail in the wall. There was something in her half-smile, and in the languid sweep of her arm as she hung the scarf, that made me say, "I'm going to take the kids to explore the town. Why don't you and Bob take a nap? You've earned it!"

They both thanked me with their eyes. Linda and Cathy and Josh were ready to stretch their legs; we shut the door behind us, heading out onto the street and up the short half block to the dusty central square. It lacked the leafy charm of the plaza in San Ignacio, but there were a few benches inhabited by a few locals, and on a makeshift basketball court, a handful of youths leaped and shouted exuberantly.

Turning down a narrow side lane, we passed the town laundromat: a pale blue house with barred windows, one room open to the street and containing two Bendix washers set between a green velvet sofa and matching armchair. Next door to the laundromat was the *tortillería*. We could hear the soft *slap-slap* of a woman's hands shaping tortillas and could smell the tantalizing scent of fresh *masa*.

"I'm stawved!" cried Josh, suddenly. I remembered a little restaurant next to the hotel, and we headed back that way. Just beside the restaurant was a small general store, no more than the front room of someone's house, with a glass case inside the doorway displaying pinwheel lollipops and old comic books. The kids swerved in, discussing the lollipops in hushed, urgent tones. Behind the counter, the proprietor smiled at them, then turned to me.

"Hello, lady," he said in English. "How you are?"

I returned his smile. "Fine, thank you," I answered. "How are you?"

"I very happy to have so pretty lady and so nice kids in my store." He looked about sixty, stout and cheerful, with black hair slicked back in waves and a thin black mustache. "Where you from?"

"From California."

"I live for tree years in Hollywood. Long time ago. I espeak pretty good English."

"Yes," I agreed, "your English is fine."

The children were clamoring for candy. I pointed to the lollilops through the glass and held up three fingers. The man bent down and slid open the backdoor of the case, pulling out the lollipops. When he straightened up, he held the candy in his left hand; in his right, he held a small guitar.

"Listen!" he commanded. "I sing you!"

He leaned back and began strumming, the sound tinny but enthusiastic. He sang:

> *Five foot two*
> *Eyes of blue*
> *Oh what those two eyes can do—*
> *Has anybody seen my gal?*

I threw back my head and laughed so hard I had to sit down on the curb. The kids looked from me to the singer and back again in astonishment, lollipops momentarily forgotten.

"Thank you!" I said, rising and wiping my eyes. "What's your name?"

"Armando Miguel Gómez Portillo, at your service." He extended his hand across the counter. As I reached over to take it, I glanced down. Armando, beneath his elegant pearl-gray *guayabera*, was wearing only a pair of boxer shorts. He kissed my hand, and I ushered the children out, shaking my head and chuckling.

When we returned to the Vieja Hacienda after lunch, we found Sue sunning herself on one of the wooden chairs in the courtyard, a pink hibiscus blossom in her hair. Bob was just emerging from the room looking rumpled but happy. The tension between them had dissolved completely.

I told them about my encounter in the little store.

"Oh," said Sue, "you must have met Armando!"

"You know him?"

"We met him three years ago, when we came here for the first time," said Bob. "We gave him some old Playboy magazines we had brought to trade for food and stuff. He was really happy to get those magazines."

Sue laughed. "You know what he said? He said, 'I will delight myself tonight!'" She rubbed her hands together gleefully, in imitation of Armando's gesture. "Was he wearing pants today?"

Linda had brought out a deck of cards from the room, and the children were playing Go Fish at one of the little tables in the shade.

"Let's get a beer," suggested Bob.

Just across the courtyard was a long, low structure, once an outbuilding of the hacienda, that had been converted into a cantina with a long bar and several round tables set with mismatched chairs. Before the advent of the paved road, Mulegé had been the private haunt of a few bush pilots who flew their small craft over the jungle of palm trees to the primitive landing strip still visible on a mesa across town. Alfonso, the owner of the Vieja Hacienda, was himself a pilot, and was often away on his own adventures. The regulars in his bar were accustomed to helping themselves to drinks in Alfonso's absence. Payment was on an honor system—the money was deposited in an unlocked box by a bottle of Bacardi. Into the polished wood of the bar, generations of adventurers had carved their names.

The only other drinker that afternoon was Mario, a friend of Alfonso, who was looking after things while Alfonso spent the New Year's holiday with friends in La Paz. It was Mario who had checked us in and who now served us our Tecates.

"Tomorrow's New Year's Eve," observed Bob. "What's going on in town, Mario?"

"There's a big dinner and dance at the Hotel Serenidad," Mario said. 'They're charging thirty-five dollars per person. Otherwise, there's just a lot of private parties."

"Hmm," murmured Sue, running her finger around the rim of her glass. "Thirty-five dollars a person is beyond our budget." She smiled warmly at Bob. I felt a momentary pang of envy for the comfortable intimacy that had replaced their earlier hostility. I guessed its source.

"We could crash one of the parties," I suggested. I had never crashed a party in my life, but the beer, and a growing sense of solitude, had made me feel reckless.

"I have an idea," Bob said, passing his empty can to Mario who exchanged it for a full one. "Mario, do you think Alfonso would mind if we made our own party here? I think I can get some music"— Bob indicated an old radio on the shelf behind the bar—"and we'll replace whatever we drink. It might even bring in some more customers!"

Sue had pulled the hibiscus out of her hair in her excitement and waved it at Mario. "We could get candles and streamers at Armando's store," she exclaimed, "and put bougainvillea on the tables . . . "

Mario shrugged, palms turned upward, in the Mexican equivalent of "OK."

"Come on." Sue took my arm, pulling me gently off the bar stool. "Let's check out Armando's now, while Bob finishes his beer. Keep an eye on the kids," she called back, as we hurried out.

Armando greeted me as though I were his long-lost lover, and claimed to remember Sue from three years before. He entertained us with a garbled version of "Dark Town Strutters' Ball" while we collected the makings of a party: two dozen votive candles, strips of colored crepe paper, ten bags of peanuts. As we were taking our leave, Sue asked, "Where are the clams this year, Armando?"

"Still at Requesón Beach, *señora*," he answered with a gallant bow.

"That's what we'll have for our New Year's Eve dinner," Sue told me firmly, taking my elbow and guiding me down the street, "piles of fresh steamed clams!"

To that end, we all climbed into the van the next morning, taking with us the tin bucket that held some of the firewood in our room. Requesón is actually an island south of Mulegé, connected to the beach by a long sand spit. The tide was out when we got there, and the sand spit was easy to see. The kids peeled off their clothes down to the bathing suits they wore underneath. Bob and Sue and I rolled up the cuffs of our sweatpants.

"Curl your toes under in the wet sand," Bob called out. "You'll feel the clams' shells."

The sea shone smooth and as still as blue satin. The sun, almost directly overhead, was like a warm embrace, and the water felt soft. For a while we all just kicked our feet around, splashing in pure sensual delight.

"Hey!" yelled Linda, suddenly. "I found one!" She was on her knees in the shallow water, digging furiously. Bob hurried over and pushed his own hand deep into the sand where Linda had made a hole. When he arose, he held up a big clam, five or six inches across.

"Mine!" cried Linda.

"Ours," declared Bob, dropping it in the bucket.

After that, everyone began finding clams, even little Josh, and soon the bucket was almost full. The kids looked like sea creatures, soaked and caked with sand from head to toe. There was no one on the beach, or on the island; our only companions were the gulls and sandpipers competing with us for the clams. I felt wonderful, salty and damp and wild. Then, from out of nowhere, the wind began to blow, raising whitecaps and sending little waves scuttling over the sand spit.

"Here comes the wind," called Sue. "Let's get out of here!"

I would learn over and over again, in the years ahead, to respect the Baja wind. That afternoon, within ten minutes, it had us all sprinting for the van, shivering and clutching our wet clothes around us. By the time we got back to the hotel, Josh was huddled on my lap, lips turning blue with cold, and Cathy and Linda were pressed up against me in two miserable little bundles. The so-called hot water in the Vieja Hacienda came on at 3:00 each afternoon and lasted till 4:00; it was now only 2:15. But Bob quickly built a big fire, and we put on dry clothes and toasted ourselves in its glow.

"I still have a chill in my bones," said Sue. She disappeared for a few minutes and returned from the bar with a bottle of tequila, a salt shaker, limes, and three glasses. We warmed ourselves inside and out until the hot-water hour; then, although the water was only lukewarm, we all took our time in the shower, rinsing off the sand while mesquite wood filled our little room with fragrant heat.

Afterward we steamed the clams in one of our big camping pots over the fire, flavoring the broth with basil from the courtyard garden, limes from the bar, and Señora Duarte's chiles. The meal was sumptuous, sensuous, delicious, and soon the low wooden table we had hauled in from outside was piled with discarded shells, loose change, spicy lime juice, and empty soda bottles. The little girls were reading on the bed while we grown-ups sprawled in total contentment before the fire, embraced by a haze of warmth and tequila and clams. Only Josh was restless, wandering around the room looking for action. He picked up a loose peso from the table, put it in his mouth. I was slow to react.

"Joshie," I murmured, "you know you're not supposed to put coins in your mouth."

But Josh had already spit the peso onto the floor. His eyes were huge and watery, and he was gasping like a dying fish.

"Hot!" he sputtered. "That peso was hot!"

All of the loose change on the table was bathed in a soup of lime juice and chile that dripped through the wood slats. I put my arm around Josh, and Sue brought the carafe of drinking water from the bathroom. After a few minutes the crisis passed.

"Well, Josh," I said, feeling vaguely guilty for my little son's suffering, "I hope you learned something."

"Yeah," said Josh, earnestly, "I'll nevuh suck on *that* peso again!"

When the light outside began to deepen to a purple glow, we all crossed the courtyard to the cantina, bearing our booty from Armando's store. Cathy and Linda brought in bougainvillea blossoms and arranged them on all the tables and along the bar. Sue dripped wax onto saucers and placed a candle in the middle of each flower arrangement. Josh and I hung streamers of crepe paper, green and white and red, along the walls, while Bob used a metal coat hanger to augment the radio's antenna and managed to find a station that came in well enough to hear. By the time we had finished, it was dark. Sue and I lit all the candles, and the room seemed to float in flowers and soft light and music.

"Wow!" breathed Linda, "it's beautiful!"

"It's just like in *Sara Crewe*," Cathy whispered, referring to the Frances Hodgson Burnett book she was reading. She slipped her hand into mine, and I gave it a squeeze.

Josh just stood there, eyes shining. I stooped down and put an arm around his shoulder; he turned and hugged me hard around the neck. He smelled like limes and like the ocean.

Then we all sat down at one of the tables and passed around Pepsis.

"Happy New Year!" said Bob, raising his Pepsi in a toast. We clinked bottles. Then, in a rush of uncharacteristic spontaneity, I got up and went around the table, hugging everyone. I couldn't even remember what I had done the previous New Year's Eve, but I was already sure that this was better.

Armando must have spread the word, because our little party attracted a modest crowd of locals, mostly older teens escaping late from family gatherings and looking for somewhere else to go. One boy brought a guitar and provided a few hours of live music. A middle-aged American couple, tourists from Arizona, stopped in off the street. Just before midnight, two women about my age, both hearing-impaired and traveling together through Baja, joined us. One of them had lost her hearing from disease, around puberty; having once heard, she was able to lip-read and to speak, so we could communicate. Their courage, and all the general good fellowship around me, put my earlier feelings of solitude into perspective. By the time the radio announcer shouted, "*¡Feliz Año Nuevo!*" I was hardly feeling sorry for myself at all and only thought once of Carlos.

January 2 was our planned departure date. Bob and Sue were eager to spend at least one night on Bahía Concepción, which they remembered fondly from their previous trip, so by noon on New Year's Day we were heading south in the van, feeling remarkably fine. In about twenty minutes we turned onto Santispac Beach, a long crescent of white sand enclosing a bay of shimmering turquoise. We had our pick of camping spots and parked by a cluster of palm trees. The children hit the water immediately with their masks and snorkels, splashing out toward the mangrove swamp across the inlet where, Bob told me, oysters grew in abundance.

"There's something else in that mangrove swamp, too," Sue confided to me. "A secret hot spring that the Indians used to use. I think I could find it again. Want to try?"

"I'm game," I said. "Does Bob mind watching the kids?"

"No, Bob doesn't mind," said Bob, grinning wryly at me. "Go on."

I had no idea how Sue knew where she was going as she wove through the tangled brush and roots at the far end of the beach. We were soon out of sight of the van and the palm trees.

"Here it is!" she cried. Hidden in a cover of vines and leaves was a small pool, maybe five feet wide, into which had been sunk a huge copper pot, like the one the *carnitas* had cooked in at the Tijuana restaurant. The pot was filled with slightly muddy, steaming water. I slipped out of my thongs and stepped in. Sue had already stripped off her bathing suit and was wallowing like a pink hippo. The water was hot, probably a little over a hundred degrees, and smelled of sulfur. It seemed to permeate my pores; I was sure it must have curative powers. Sue reached over the edge of the pot and scooped up a handful of warm mud.

"Beauty treatment," she sighed happily, smearing the mud on her face. "Try it. Best mudpack in town."

By the time we got back to camp, we looked like a couple of otters, slick with mud and steaming. Bob had snorkeled out with the kids and gathered oysters for our supper, and while Sue and I rinsed off in the bay, he started a campfire with wood we had brought from the hotel. We sautéed the oysters in olive oil and garlic, and even the children devoured them eagerly.

That night, Bob and Sue pitched a tent for themselves and Linda. Cathy and Josh and I slept in the van. I had just finished setting up our bed and was coming across to the Shaffers' tent to say good-night, when I noticed something shining in the dark water. There was no moon, but with each little wave that rolled in, the sea sparkled with a silver light. Bob had noticed it, too.

"It's phosphorescence," he explained, "microscopic sea creatures that glow in the dark. Look." He waded a few yards out and dipped his hand in the water. His hand lit up. Then we were all dipping our hands, then our arms, and soon we were all swimming, gliding about in the warm blackness, our bodies radiant.

Later, drowsy and dry under the quilt, I asked Cathy and Josh, "How do you feel?" But they were both already asleep. When I looked down at their soft faces, I thought they were still glowing.

It was early when I woke up, and the only sound in the morning stillness was the soft *plop-plop* of little fish jumping by the shore. When I peeked out the open back door of the van, I saw an opalescent world: sea and sky merged in shades of soft pink and blue and pearly white, like the inside of an abalone shell, forming an arch of radiance all around us. Then I saw Bob and Sue emerge silently from their tent; their backs were to me, and they were holding hands, looking into each other's eyes. Without a word, they moved together down the beach, their naked bodies gleaming white. They slid soundlessly into the water and, for a long moment, seemed to disappear into the luminescence. By the time I could see them again, the sun was up, and they were laughing and grabbing for towels, and it was time to leave.

Mulegé and Bahía Concepción would never be the same again. By 1984, the blossoms and wild basil at the Vieja Hacienda had been replaced by a swimming pool, and a new section of rooms had been added, modeled after a Travelodge. By 1987, Santispac Beach resembled a parking lot for RVs. We would never again swim in such luminescence or in such an innocent dawn.

Ejido Eréndira

Ya viene amaneciendo,
ya la luz el día nos dió.
Levántate de mañana;
mira que ya amaneció.

Now is the dawn approaching;
now is the day's light given to us.
Arise in the morning;
behold what has just dawned!

—Traditional Mexican birthday song, "Las Mañanitas"

I t smells like a Mexican kitchen in here!" Carlos was chuckling as he sidled up behind me and hugged my waist.

"Happy birthday," I said, turning from the stove. "Taste." I held out a wooden spoon full of hot beans. Carlos tasted and smacked his lips with exaggerated glee.

"*Perfecto*," he announced. "As good as my mother's."

"Liar," I said, and turned back to the stove where pots steamed on all four burners.

Cathy and Josh sat at the kitchen table sipping Pepsis and slicing carrots for the *sopa de arroz*. Josh asked, "How old are you going to be today, Carlos?"

"Twenty-one," answered Carlos, helping himself to a swig of Josh's Pepsi.

"No way, José!" Josh pushed his chair back, stood up, and reached for the Pepsi that Carlos was holding up, out of reach.

"You mean, 'No way, Josué,'" said Carlos, swinging the Pepsi can down on the table behind Josh and throwing a gentle punch at the boy's shoulder.

In the fourteen months since we had returned from Mulegé, Carlos had gradually become a regular fixture in our kitchen, sometimes dropping by with Jorge, but more and more often coming over alone for a cup of coffee or a meal. As our daily lives had begun to intertwine, Carlos had given us all Spanish names, as if doing so made us more real to him. Cathy, of course, became *Catarina*, but he called her *Fresita*, Little Strawberry, for her pink cheeks and freckles. Joshua translated into *Josué* or its diminutive, *Josuito*.

My name was more problematic for Carlos. At first, when he and I were taking care to maintain a safe psychological distance between us, he simply called me "Hey Goldstein," or sometimes "Doc." Then one July weekend when Cathy and Josh were with their dad, Carlos invited me to join him for a weekend camping trip to a beach south of Tijuana known as La Salina.

It was during that weekend that Carlos found a name for me. After crossing the border, we had driven along the rugged Baja coast for forty miles until the jagged cliffs gave way to a stretch of wide sandy beach. Accustomed to San Diego's crowded, developed beaches, I had looked around for the parking lot and the lifeguard stand, and had been startled when Carlos pulled right onto the sand and parked. The beach stretched south for perhaps two miles; I could make out only three other vehicles besides our own. There was no lifeguard stand or concession stand, there were no beach umbrellas or volleyball nets, and the only sound was the low boom and hiss of the surf. I climbed down from the van and inhaled the sharp sweet air. A few yards away, a flock of gulls stood motionless, staring out to sea as though watching a distant shore invisible to us. Just beyond the birds, a jumble of dark lava rock reached out into the water for a hundred yards, forming a natural jetty. To the east, on the other side of the road, brown hills piled up against a blaze of blue sky. Clinging to the slope of one of the hills, beside a lone shack of faded red planks, sprawled a solitary field of corn, its vigorous green stalks raised like defiant fists against the relentless sun.

Carlos was busy unloading the van: two folding beach chairs, firewood, a cooler, and his fishing pole. "Well, Doc," he said, "you're home! How do you like it?"

"Too crowded," I replied. Then he chased me into the water, and then we were both diving through the surf, our wet clothes billowing around us, until finally, soaked and sandy, we struggled back to the beach, grateful for its solid warmth.

By late afternoon the tide was low enough that we could explore almost the whole length of the jetty without fear of being swept away. The tide pools teemed with silent drama: a juvenile garabaldi flashed turquoise past a purple sea urchin whose dangerous spines hid its delicate inner flesh. Nearby, a tiny pink crab, no bigger than a thumbnail, scuttled past a sea anemone whose translucent sapphire arms swayed hypnotically, urging the little fellow into its soft, deadly maw. As I watched the pulsing life of the tide pool, I could feel the sun beating hot on my face and on my thighs and could taste the salt on my lips. I thought I could even feel the heat reflected from Carlos's body. He bent beside me over the edge of a rock, patiently prying away the slick black mussels he used for bait. His smooth back, glistening with sweat and sea spray, was the same tawny gold as the lowering sun. He glanced over his shoulder at me as though he had felt my eyes. Then he sat back and reached out to touch my tousled hair.

"*Mirasol*," he said softly. I watched his eyes for a clue. They glowed like molten bronze. "It means Sunflower," he said. "You look like a sunflower. *Mira el sol* : Looks-at-the-sun."

"Just now," I said, "the sun I was looking at was you."

But Carlos only called me Mirasol in private. Among family, he called me Judith, giving it the Spanish pronounciation: "Hoodeet." Now, in our kitchen, while Cathy and Josh set the table, he emphasized the hoot. "Hoody!" he yelled, and both children chanted "hoody, hoody, hoody," as they bore steaming bowls from stove to table.

I had prepared what I hoped was a festive Mexican meal: chicken with *mole* sauce, refried beans, *sopa de arroz*, and hot tortillas. When I had asked my clinic patients for their recipes for *mole*, all of the younger women had laughed and told me that they used Doña Maria's canned *mole* sauce. The older *señoras* each had her own version of the recipe, but all the recipes included chocolate, chiles, nuts, and various seeds.

"Chocolate and chiles?" I had asked Sue incredulously, when I first learned of the ingredients. "Together? On *chicken*?"

Sue had shrugged. "It's an Aztec dish," she told me. "Cocoa beans were a delicacy. And they certainly had lots of chiles."

And lots of time. Everyone's recipe was highly labor-intensive, involving hours of peeling and grinding and blending. Driving home from the clinic in rush-hour traffic, I tried to imagine myself as an Aztec woman. I kept my own green eyes and tawny hair, but I colored my skin a rich golden-brown. Then I filled out my skinny limbs and small breasts until I looked as lush as a ripe mango. I left my new bosom bare, but around my waist I wound—what did Aztec women wear, anyway? I didn't know, but I mentally sketched in a short skirt woven with geometric shapes of orange and green. Finally, I stuck a peacock feather in my hair, and visualized myself kneeling outside a mud hut, grinding cocoa, chiles, and mountains of seeds on a grinding stone worn smooth with use. I was chattering happily with three or four other women who were also grinding away on their *morteros*. It looked like a scene from a very bad movie, and I burst out laughing all alone in my car. When I got off the freeway, I stopped at López Market on the edge of town and bought two jars of Doña Maria's canned *mole* sauce.

I wasn't sure how authentic the meal really was, but it was certainly festive. Bob and Sue brought a couple of bottles of wine from the Santo Tomás vineyards, and Jorge brought his guitar. We all serenaded Carlos with "*Las Mañanitas*," the Mexican birthday song. For dessert, Cathy brought out a lemon cake she had made herself. It had thirty-seven candles on it, and when Carlos blew them out he held both children on his lap.

It was late when everyone finally left. Cathy and Josh had fallen asleep on the living room carpet listening to "*La Llorona*," and Carlos carried them to their beds. Then he followed me out to the kitchen. I began washing dishes, and he started scrubbing the stove, his back to me.

"Carlitos is coming for spring break," he said.

Carlitos, known as Charley to everyone but his dad, was Carlos's twelve-year-old son. He had moved to San Francisco with his mother when she remarried, but he usually visited Carlos during school vacations. I knew how much Carlos missed him.

"I thought maybe I'd take him fishing," Carlos was saying. He was bent over the stove, attacking it with his sponge as if he expected it to fight back.

I said, "Mmmm."

"I thought maybe Josuito would like to come with us," Carlos continued, scrubbing harder.

I rinsed a plate and then stood still, my hands in the soapy water. I was thinking about the green marble Carlitos had given Josh the previous summer, a special variety that the kids called a "cleary." Josh kept it in an old cigar box with his Ozzie Smith baseball card and his Luke Skywalker medallion.

Carlos went over to the table and sat down, still gripping his sponge. I turned toward him and was startled by the pleading in his eyes.

"That little *chavo* needs to learn to fish," he said. "I'd love to teach him." I came over to the table and sat down beside him, reaching for his hand. "I want to show the boys Eréndira," Carlos continued, looking at me earnestly. "Remember Ejido Eréndira?"

"Yes," I said softly. "I remember."

We had left the paved highway about forty-five miles south of Ensenada, turning west onto a narrow dirt road that was scarred with deep ruts from the previous winter's rains. At first the road wound through a shady canyon where sycamores swayed over a bright little stream. But soon the stream curved away, and we entered a country of low hills covered with dry scrub. As we rattled slowly through the monotonous landscape, the August air heavy with resinous scents and humming with insect sounds, I began to lose my bearings. The same brown hills rolled away forever in all directions, featureless against a blank sky. Only a pale glow, a kind of shining mantle floating over the farthest hills, told me that we were headed west toward the sea. In the midday heat, it seemed that nothing at all was moving except our van, and the going was so slow along the rough dirt trail that even the van seemed almost motionless.

Suddenly, far ahead, I saw a tiny puff of smoke rise into the air. As it moved toward us, it grew into a cloud of brown dust, followed by the noise of a motor. Carlos pulled the van off the road onto a flat patch of chaparral, and an ancient pickup truck clattered by, its bed loaded with tomatoes. The driver wore a battered straw cowboy hat and a red bandanna around his neck. As he passed, he raised his hand in greeting and smiled.

Pulling back onto the road, Carlos said, "That guy's bringing tomatoes from the *ejido*. Probably going to sell them in Ensenada."

"What's an *ejido*?" I asked.

"It's like a collective farm," answered Carlos. Then I heard the first of what would eventually be dozens of versions of the story of *La Revolución*. I heard about the rich *hacendados* who, by the turn of the century, owned ninety-seven percent of Mexico's land although they comprised only a few families. I heard how the *campesinos* rose up in 1910 with the cry of "*¡Tierra y libertad!*" on their lips. And I heard how they won that land and liberty despite impossible odds, despite hunger and poverty, despite the Mexican *federales*, despite even the powerful gringos who sent an army across the border in search of Pancho Villa, the revolutionary hero. I heard about agrarian reform, institutionalized in Article 27 of the new Revolutionary Constitution, guaranteeing that the land would henceforth belong to those who worked it for the good of *la república*. I heard . . .

"Carlos!" I cried. "Look!"

We had crested another hill, and there, on the far horizon, the ocean sparkled like a sudden smile. As if a curtain had parted, the air cooled and a little breeze sprang up.

The road leveled out and wound around the base of a high, rocky cliff on our right. On our left, the stream had reappeared; it flashed and murmured beside us like an eager guide. Presently we came to a cluster of houses, too few to constitute a village, but enough to be a settlement. Carlos stopped the van in front of a ramshackle wooden house whose once-white paint was faded to a weathered, peeling gray. Three skinny dogs appeared out of nowhere and stopped a few feet from us, barking excitedly. A woman in a shapeless, colorless dress rounded the corner of the house, wiping her hands on a grimy apron. Judging by her dark hair and intact dentition, she was probably in her early forties, but her brown face was deeply lined.

"*Buenas tardes, señora*," Carlos called.

She peered at him, squinting, then broke into a smile.

"*¡Qué tal, Carlos! ¿Cómo has estado?*"

They embraced, kissing each other lightly on the cheek. Then Carlos introduced me, and the woman shook my hand shyly.

"*¿Y El Rey, señora? No está?*" According to my mental translation, Carlos was inquiring as to the whereabouts of The King. I figured I must have misunderstood.

"No," answered the woman in Spanish. "El Rey went out to fish early this morning. He's not back yet." The King again. I hadn't misunderstood.

"Well," said Carlos, "greet him for me, if you please, *señora*. Maybe I'll see him on the way back."

"Wouldn't you like to come in and wait for him?" asked the woman. I wondered if she was The Queen. "Perhaps I can offer you something to drink . . . "

"Maybe on the way back," said Carlos politely. "I promised *la doctora* I would show her your beautiful beach."

"*Andale,*" said The Queen. "*Vayanse con Dios.*"

"The King?" I asked as we bounced across a small bridge over the stream. "Who's The King?"

Carlos laughed. "El Rey? He's the son of Jorge's cousin's sister-in-law. He and his brother have a *panga....* "

"What's a *panga?*"

" It's a fishing boat, kind of like a Boston Whaler. They're great for getting out through the surf. Anyway, El Rey fishes around here, knows the good spots. He took me out with him about five years ago, and we filled the boat with corvina in a couple of hours."

"That woman acted as if she's known you for years."

"That's El Rey's mother. She cooked up our fish for us, and we all had a meal together five years ago. Not much happens around here, so I guess I was a big event. Besides, I'm practically family since I'm a friend of Jorge's, and he's a relative of El Rey."

"Pretty distant relative," I observed dryly. "Why do they call him El Rey?"

"*¿Quién sabe?*" said Carlos. "Why do you ask so many questions?"

We had left the houses behind. Just ahead rose a grove of olive trees, silvery against the deep, clean blue of the ocean. To the east stretched long rows of green tomato plants, their red fruit dark against the darker brown earth. Along the rows, men and women bent and swayed rhythmically, moving slowly through the fields like ambulatory flowers, their heads swathed against the sun in bright-hued shirts and scarves. As the van lumbered past, they straightened and waved.

Why *did* I ask so many questions? I felt my compulsive need to know drift away like dust across the peaceful fields. From my open window I gazed out on a long curve of beach cradled beneath craggy cliffs. In the distance, the sun and the sky and the sea receded into a shining, insubstantial mist. There were no other campers anywhere in sight.

Carlos pulled the van out onto the wide cliff ledges that overlooked the beach, one after another. On each ledge, he would get out, watch the ocean for a time, scan the beach, and then drive on. Finally he settled on a low ledge protected by a rocky outcropping and graced by a sweeping view of the coast. After he had moved the van back and forth a few times—positioning it to minimize the inevitable wind—he scrambled down to the beach, shed his clothes, and dove into the surf. I pulled one of the folding chairs from the back of the van and settled down, watching Carlos plow through the waves to the calmer water beyond, a tiny speck in a vast sea.

Suddenly there was another swimmer with him, a large shape in a black wetsuit. I assumed it was a surfer and wondered where he had come from; I hadn't seen any signs of any other campers. I was still musing on the mysterious surfer when Carlos materialized beside me, naked and dripping wet, clutching his clothes. He was breathing hard.

"That was fast," I observed. "I just saw you talking to that surfer out there. Where's his camp?"

"¡Híjole!" Carlos swore. "That surfer's a sea lion. ¡Un lobo del mar muy grande! He came over to check me out."

I looked again. The sea lion hovered just beyond the breakers—massive, motionless, watching us with what I imagined to be a mixture of curiosity and suspicion. Carlos grabbed a towel from the van and wrapped it around his waist. The thought of suave Carlos beating a fast retreat across the waves like a big flying fish struck me funny. I started to laugh, and Carlos grinned sheepishly.

"Hell," he said. "It's his barrio, and he outweighs me by at least a ton. Sometimes a man's just gotta know when to walk away!"

"You call that walking?" I said, and giggled at my own joke.

Carlos swatted at me playfully with his towel. "Don't gimme no lip, Woman," he said. "Go make yourself useful."

I pulled the other beach chair from the van and unfolded it for Carlos. Then I opened the cooler and brought out two cold beers. We clinked cans.

"To machismo," I said, kidding. Carlos was serious. He raised his beer toward the ocean, saluting the sea lion.

"To the *lobo*," he said. "*Mis respetos*."

When we emerged from the van the next morning, the sea lion was gone. But just below us, in the emerald waves near shore, a group of dolphins dove and splashed exuberantly. We sipped our coffee and watched them play, half-convinced that they were showing off for our benefit. After a while, we ventured down to the beach and slid into the water ourselves, some fifty yards north of our companions. They seemed unconcerned by our presence, and one of the smaller ones even leaped straight up out of the water as if in welcome. There was no need for bathing suits, and the cool water enveloped my body like a caress. I wished for the fins and muscles of a dolphin so that I, too, could leap and dive my joy.

In the afternoon, Carlos walked down the beach to where a low shelf of rock reached out to sea. He carried a long fishing pole and a worn metal tackle box. I trailed along behind, gathering shells along the water's edge. When I caught up with him, he was already reeling in his line. As it surfaced, I saw a little fish thrashing desperately against the hook. Carlos laid the fish on a flat rock and used a needle-nose pliers to free the hook from its mouth. Then he grasped the fish in his hand and held it up. The fish's eyes seemed to widen as I watched, and its mouth opened and closed spasmodically.

Carlos peered into the fish's face.

"You dumb little *cabrón*, don't you know a fish hook when you see one?" He spoke gently, almost tenderly. "Now let this be a lesson to you! Don't make the same mistake again." With a low sweep of his arm, he tossed the fish back into the sea, clear of the rocks. The fish just hung there in the water for a moment, stunned, then wriggled its tail and disappeared. Carlos looked at me, shrugging apologetically.

"Too small," he explained. "Besides, that kind of fish doesn't make very good eating."

"What kind was it?" I asked. I had never seen anyone catch a fish before, and my heart was pounding with a strange excitement.

"Perch," Carlos answered shortly. He was already baiting his hook again with the glistening pink meat of a mussel he had pried from the rock beside us. "Corvina's better," he added, and cast his line in a long, graceful arc. I watched the bait sail out over the water for a long way before it finally floated down and sank out of sight.

"Here," said Carlos, handing me the pole. "The next fish is yours."

"But I don't . . . "

He laughed. "All you have to do is stand there and hold it," he said.

"How will I know if I have a fish?" I asked. I could feel the swell and surge of the sea, transmitted through the rod into my hands. It seemed to flow up my arms and into my chest, where my heart was swelling and surging responsively.

"You'll feel it," Carlos said.

"But what . . . "

"Why do you ask so many questions?" he said for the second time in twenty-four hours. "Just wait. You'll know when it happens."

I was so nervous that I reeled in the line twice when there was nothing on it. The third time I felt a strong tug and was sure I had a fish, but it was only a clump of seaweed. Carlos patiently baited the hook again and cast it out, then handed me the pole.

"If we're going to eat tonight, you're going to have to catch something," he said. "I'm working up an appetite out here."

He sat down beside me and busied himself with collecting more mussels. I relaxed into a kind of trance, watching the waves roll in and out, watching the pelicans swoop and dive, feeling the steady pulse of the tide through the pole in my hands. Suddenly I felt a sharp pull on the line, and then the whole pole began to vibrate and jerk as if it had come alive. I gripped it harder.

"Fish!" I yelled. "I've got a fish!"

Carlos looked up, looked out at the line and the pole. "You sure do," he said. He stood up, legs apart, arms folded across his chest.

"Now bring it in."

"Help me, Carlos! I can't do this alone!"

"Sure you can," he said, but he came and stood behind me and laid his hands over mine. "Just turn the reel," he told me, "I'm right here."

It was a big corvina, and I brought it in myself, trembling with the deep energy of the sea, and the life energy of the fish, and the warm, strong energy of Carlos's hands on mine.

Now, sitting at my kitchen table, I gave Carlos's hand a squeeze.

"I think the boys would love Ejido Eréndira," I said. "If Josh wants to go with you guys, it's OK with me."

Carlos raised my hand to his lips and kissed it. "*Gracias*," he said.

When I told Josh about the invitation to the fishing trip, he mumbled, "Yeah, sure, I guess so." But he puffed his chest out and swaggered when he said it, and in the ensuing weeks, whenever Josh talked about the trip, his voice dropped two octaves below its normal register.

"I think I better take a fishin' hat," he told me.

"A fishing hat?" I asked. "What's that?"

"Well, Carlos and Charley both have fishin' hats," he said. "Where they stick their tackle and stuff."

"Hmm," I said. "Why don't you just wear your Padres cap?"

"Mom!" he said, disgusted.

On the first Saturday of spring break, a warm April day, I stood in my front doorway and watched Carlos and Charley pack my old sleeping bag into the van for Josh, along with his backpack stuffed with extra socks and sweatshirts. Carlos wore a floppy-brimmed khaki cap whose stained hatband sprouted feathers and rubber worms in neon yellows and greens. Charley wore a slightly newer-looking version of the same cap. Josh looked very small standing in the driveway with his Padres cap slipping down over his eyes. He was clutching a fishing pole that was at least twice as tall as he was, and he kept shifting uneasily from one foot to the other. He had never been away from me except to visit his dad or his grandparents. I blinked hard and swallowed.

Carlos came over and gave me a quick hug. "We'll see you and the little *Fresita* in a few days," he said. I had asked for the last half of the week off; Jorge was going to drive down to Ejido Eréndira on Wednesday, and Cathy and I were going to go with him. "Jorge will take good care of you," Carlos called to me as he climbed into the van. I started to retort that I could take care of myself, thank you very much, but I choked on the words. I was no longer sure they were true. Josh's small face pressed against the van's window, and he waved with a shaky smile. The VW engine coughed, sputtered, and caught, and then they were gone.

"*Vaya con Dios, Josuito,*" I heard myself murmur. Then I wiped my eyes with the corner of my T-shirt and went inside.

Jorge was the roundest person I had ever known. His face was round, his body was round, and his balding head formed a smooth globe above a circle of grizzled hair. From behind his round black-rimmed glasses, dark eyes surveyed the world with warmth, intelligence, and humor.

Although he was ten years older than Carlos, he radiated an almost adolescent innocence. Having been sent away to a seminary school when he was only nine, and having been ordained into the priesthood as a young man, Jorge had missed the worldly experiences that had shaped his roommate. Carlos sometimes treated Jorge like a kid brother, claiming that his social skills were those of a twelve-year-old. When he first left the priesthood and came to the U.S., Jorge had fallen in love with every woman who smiled at him. Twelve years later, he remained touchingly vulnerable. He nursed his frequently broken heart with tequila and Mexican love songs, which he sang with a strong voice and with that singular, heart-wrenching *grito*—simultaneously laughter and sob—that is the signature of Mexican soul.

Jorge knocked on my door at 10:00 on Wednesday morning wearing the same light blue shirt, navy blue slacks, and polished black shoes that he wore to work, to parties, and to the beach. Despite twelve years as a U.S. resident, he had remained far less Americanized than Carlos. When Cathy and I stepped out into the driveway, Jorge swept up our bags and opened the door of his truck for us, holding my elbow as I climbed into the cab. Cathy crawled happily back into the camper shell where Jorge had piled blankets and pillows for her.

"Are you comfortable, *mi reina?*" he asked her.

Cathy blushed and giggled. "I'm not a queen," she said.

"You're my little queen," Jorge said. Coming from him, it sounded sincere.

"They don't make 'em like you anymore, Jorge," I told him fondly as we drove away.

Jorge smiled his big warm smile and chuckled. Unlike Carlos, whose English was smooth and idiomatic, Jorge was still more comfortable with Spanish. He told me, "*Mi papá siempre me decía que un verdadero hombre es feo, fuerte, y formal.*" "My father used to always tell me that a real man is ugly, strong, and formal." He flexed his right arm, showing me his biceps like a little kid. I patted his knee with affection as we swung onto the freeway and headed south.

By the time we reached Ensenada, I was bristling with anticipation; we'd be there in just a couple of hours. When Jorge parked the truck in front of a grocery store, I had to stifle my impatience. Why hadn't he thought about groceries ahead of time? My own cooler had been stocked since the day before, each meal carefully packaged in its own plastic bag and pre-frozen.

Waiting in the truck for Jorge, I tried to use the delay as another lesson in how to comprehend the *copretérito*. That culture-defining tense, also called the past imperfect, was one of the aspects of Spanish grammar that continued to elude me. I had finally decided that in order to understand its use, I simply had to experience time as Mexicans seemed to experience it: not as a line along which one moved directly from point to point, but rather as a kind of eternal ocean of events in which one was always floating. In the simple past tense, or *pretérito*, an event has a definite beginning and end: *Cruzamos la frontera a las diez y estuvimos en Ensenada al mediodía.* (We crossed the border at ten, and we were in Ensenada at noon.) But in the *copretérito* an event occurs as an ongoing process with no clear end in sight: *Estábamos en Ensenada cuando Jorge fue a la tienda.* (We were being/existing in Ensenada when Jorge went to the store.) I drummed my fingers on the dashboard and waited, trying to meditate on the deeper cultural meaning of the *copretérito*.

After about twenty minutes, Jorge emerged, loaded down with bags. He smiled apologetically as he stuffed them into the already crowded, unorganized camper. When he tried to put the truck into reverse to pull out, however, his smile faded.

"Uh-oh," he said. The truck hadn't moved.

"Uh-oh what?" I asked.

"No clutch," he said.

"No clutch?" I asked.

He pumped his foot up and down several times on the clutch pedal, and I could see that it hung loose and useless.

Cathy, who had been sleeping, raised her head and knocked on the window separating the camper from the cab. I slid the window back, and she said, "What's happening?"

"Don't worry, *mi reina*," said Jorge. To me he said, "My brother lives here in Ensenada, not far. I'll call him." And for another twenty minutes, I practiced the *copretérito* again while Jorge searched the neighborhood on foot, looking for a telephone.

Roberto was just as round as Jorge but at least ten years younger. He parked his old red pickup next to Jorge's truck, and then he and Jorge stood around looking at the truck for a while, kicking its tires and conferring in low tones. Finally, Jorge opened the door to Roberto's pickup.

"You and Cathy sit in here," he said. "I'll ride in the back."

"What's happening?" I asked. I sounded like Cathy's echo.

"We'll go back to Roberto's house," said Jorge. "They're going to lend us a car. We'll pick up my truck on the way home."

"What about the clutch?" I asked.

"Don't worry," said Jorge again.

It was 1:00 in the afternoon when we got to Roberto's house, a small rectangle of cinder blocks with a well-swept dirt yard in front. Inside, the living room buzzed with round people. They all started talking at once when we came in, and there was a confusing flurry of embraces and introductions and happy Spanish exclamations. Jorge was immediately absorbed by a group of men on the sofa. Cathy and I were engulfed by a flock of women and herded into the kitchen. Something smelled very familiar. The counters were littered with peanut shells and piles of chiles and . . . *¡mole!* They were making *mole!* Instead of a *mortero* they were using an electric blender, and instead of woven skirts, they were wearing polyester slacks, but otherwise, it was as I had fantasized: the chocolate and chiles and nuts and seeds were all being mixed with liberal portions of cheerful feminine gossip. Cathy and I were seated on stools and handed a succession of clay bowls filled with hot sauces to be taste-tested on our gringo tongues. The women hovered over us as if we were rare and delicate birds, scrutinizing our reactions with amused concern.

The meal went on for over an hour, during which time an astonishing number of relatives appeared. A young woman in a business suit came in as the food was being set out on the table, and two young men carrying briefcases appeared a few minutes later. Children of varying ages ran in and out of the house, most of them dressed in school uniforms. Each child went around the table and greeted everyone with a kiss before sitting down to eat. Cathy and I were included in the kissing and conversation without question, like members of the family. I thought wryly of the yogurt and carrot sticks I ate alone at my desk on most ordinary Wednesday afternoons.

At length, Jorge pushed his chair back, patted his stomach, and nodded at me. "*Vamos*," he said. Roberto got up and handed him a set of car keys. Then everyone got up and embraced us, one by one. Jorge embraced everyone, then we got into the red pickup truck, Cathy sitting on my lap in the cab beside Jorge. As we pulled away, ten or fifteen people crowded into the dirt yard and waved until we were out of sight.

"What's your brother going to do without his truck?" I asked.

"Don't worry," said Jorge.

By the time we reached the road that ran between the beach and the tomato fields, it was almost 6:00. Of course, we had stopped to talk to El Rey and his mother. The *señora* hugged me and addressed me familiarly as *tú* on the strength of our previous meeting. The King, a distinctly unregal young man with a thick black mustache and grease under his fingernails, greeted Jorge with warm respect, calling him *profesor*. He told us that he had taken Carlos and the boys out in his *panga* the day before, and he laughed raucously, describing how Don Carlos had made the little one clean and gut his own fish. I winced.

"Oh, Jorge," I sighed, as we rolled over the bridge, "Carlos is so hard on Josh. He's just a little boy."

"*Ay, Hudicita*." Jorge used my Spanish nickname. His tone was kind, almost fatherly. Through his open window, he gestured toward a cluster of nopal cactus growing in an arroyo. Their thorny fruits, called prickly pears in California, were just turning from green to a soft golden red. "Carlos is like the nopal," Jorge said, "sharp on the outside, but tender on the inside. Don't worry."

Dear, good Jorge, I thought. *You can take the man out of the priesthood, but you can't take the priesthood out of the man*. I hugged Cathy tighter against me and sniffed, surprised at the sudden spring of tears to my eyes.

Cathy was the first one to spot the van. "There they are!" she cried and started waving excitedly out the window, although we were still almost a mile away. The van stood on a bluff overlooking the sea, a dark hulk against a violet sky. As we approached, and I saw the cozy glow of light in its windows, I felt a rush of warmth, like coming home. Then I could see three figures dancing and waving wildly. Then we were there.

The first thing I noticed was that Josh looked much taller than I remembered him. The next thing I noticed was that he was wearing Carlos's fishing hat, the chartreuse worms jiggling gaily as he jumped up and down. He threw himself into my arms with a passionate bear hug. Then he remembered himself, pulled back, and said, in a deep voice, "I caught a halibut, Mom." Suddenly, everyone was talking at once.

"Where the hell have you been?" growled Carlos. In spite of himself, he grinned at me through a four-day stubble of beard.

"*Hueles a pescado, hombre*," said Jorge embracing Carlos. "You smell like fish!"

"We busted a clutch," announced Cathy proudly.

"Whose truck is that?" asked Charley.

Josh said, "Let's eat!"

The fishermen grilled their fresh catch over a mesquite fire, and we warmed some fresh tortillas we had brought from Roberto's house. Even before the after-dinner coffee was brewed, Jorge climbed into the bed of the red pickup, lay down on a thin wool blanket, and immediately began to snore, his hands folded over his belly and his shiny black shoes pointing heavenward. Carlos and I sipped warm coffee while the kids traded adventure stories, and then Charley and Josh headed off to the tent they had been sharing. Half an hour later, Carlos joined them, leaving the van to Cathy and me.

I awoke in the middle of the night to the howl of a coyote somewhere in the distance. The night smelled of something sharp, like silver, and the air seemed to vibrate. I crawled from under the warm quilt and slipped out into the chilly darkness. The sky was pulsing with stars, so close that I thought I could hear them singing across the lonely reaches of space. But as I crept down the bluff to the beach, away from camp, I realized that the song I was hearing was coming from the sea. The waves foamed and lapped at the shore, ghostly white in the starlight. Beyond lay a world of blackness, and somewhere in that blackness, the sea lion was barking. For a long time, I sat on a rock and listened to that hoarse, wild *grito*, flung across the sea to the beach, echoing from rock to rock, filling the night. It seemed to surround me until I could hear nothing else but its urgent call, intimate and strange, familiar and foreign, like an ancient and long-forgotten siren song.

San Ignacio

En el nombre del cielo
os pido posada,
porque no puede andar
mi esposa amada.

In the name of Heaven
I beg you grant us lodging,
for my beloved wife
can travel no farther.

—Traditional Mexican Christmas song, "Las Posadas"

In the weeks and months that followed, the voice of the *lobo* haunted my dreams and echoed through my days like the footsteps of an unseen companion. But little by little, other sounds intruded—the telephone's incessant ring, the roar of freeway traffic, the buzz of my busy clinic—until I could no longer recall exactly what it was I had heard that night in Eréndira.

Encarnación Mendoza appeared in the waiting room of the clinic one day wearing an embroidered white blouse of her native Oaxaca and, on her feet, green rubber thongs from Kmart. I found her planted in the middle of the room like a pyramid, her solid form immobile over wide-spread legs and her long dark hair cascading down from a smooth brow. She held the hand of a little girl who wore a pink organdy dress of ruffles and bows with a matching pink ribbon in her hair. I saw at once that the little girl had the features of Down Syndrome.

In my office, Señora Mendoza explained that she had carried Esperanza, her daughter, all the way from their small *ranchito* near the Guatemalan border to Oaxaca's capital city, seeking medical help. But the doctors in the city had told her they had no cure for Down Syndrome. So she had sold her crop of beans at the local market and had set out north with Esperanza, never doubting that the doctors *en el otro lado* could make the little girl well.

She had traveled for many weeks, riding on buses when she could and walking when she had to. She had given the last of her money to a *pollero* in Tijuana who promised to smuggle her safely across the borderline. However, when the appointed night came, she and her child waited in vain for the *pollero* to show up. Finally, just before dawn, she joined a group of young men who agreed to show her the way. They crawled on their bellies, hid in ditches, ran crouching beneath the sweep of searchlights, and all the time Encarnación held her daughter close and murmured to her gently, fearing she would cry and give them away.

Finally—trembling with terror, hungry, homesick, and penniless—Encarnación had found herself on the other side, staring at an enormously wide highway where cars flew by at impossible speeds. One of the young men who had helped her cross over had a sister in northern San Diego County. He brought Encarnación to his sister, who took her in and fed her and told her about our clinic. And now she was here at last, and I was the *doctora* she had come so far to find.

I stared out the window by my desk for a long time, watching the play of light and shadow in a pepper tree. How could I explain Down Syndrome to this woman when she lacked the basic concepts necessary to understand cells and chromosomes? How could I tell her that I had no magic? I smiled ruefully to myself, thinking of all the gringos who jam the border every weekend, heading south to Mexico in search of the magic cure for our modern malaise. And what would the Mexicans say to us? That they have no magic, either. That they cannot explain their special knowledge to us any more easily than I could explain genetics to Señora Mendoza.

In the end, we enrolled Esperanza in a special education class and helped her get the hearing aids and eyeglasses she needed. Encarnación found work caring for the children of a local family who provided a room for her and her daughter. On her days off, she would sometimes come to see me with medicinal gifts: *té de manzanilla*, chamomile tea, for my eyes, puffy from insomnia and myopia; *zábila* leaves, aloe vera, for my sunburn. I would ask her how Esperanza was doing, and she would always reply, "*Muy bien, doctora, gracias a Dios.*" Then, with patient forbearance, she would ask me when I was going to give her child the medicine that would cure her.

Although I had no cure for Down Syndrome, it was easy enough to treat the routine coughs and colds and sore throats. And as I wrote prescriptions and peered down throats, I heard the stories: a bean crop destroyed by too much rain, or too little; a baby dead of dehydration; a widowed mother; a father crippled by years of labor over a hand-held plow. Most of the men and women I saw had come north for the work, for the dollars, to feed their children, to survive. But some, especially some of the dashing young men, had come for the pure adventure, because it was there: *El Norte,* whose glittering mystique was fabled in Mexican villages as once the golden cities of Moctezuma were fabled in the towns of Spain. Those young warriors considered the border's challenges to be rites-of-passage, and their stories of danger met and mastered became their badges of honor, endowing the storyteller with romance, mystery and stature.

Near the end of June, we organized a health fair on the grounds outside the clinic. Our main purpose was to introduce our services to newcomers—those who had just arrived in the area for the agricultural season. But a second purpose was to bring the community together from their far-flung orchards and fields: information was shared along with tamales and tortas, and social bonds were forged or strengthened.

Cathy and Josh helped stuff the piñata with candy, and Sue helped me hang it from a branch of the old pepper tree. The children, dozens of them, formed a noisy, disorderly line. Each, in turn, would be blindfolded, spun around, then handed a baseball bat with which to beat at the air around the piñata. Eventually, someone would score a direct hit, and the broken piñata would rain candy onto the ground while the children converged in a squealing, greedy swarm. Inexperienced as they were, I knew Cathy and Josh didn't stand a chance, but they joined the mob and took their turns anyway.

Two boys in the crowd caught my attention. They were older and taller than the rest of the children, and they conversed quietly, set apart by their size and by a kind of serious air about them. I overheard one of the boys ask the other, "*¿Cómo te llamas?*" "What's your name?" "Pancho," replied the second boy. "*Me llamo Pancho.*"

"*¿Y en la escuela cómo te llaman?*" asked the first boy. "What's your name at school?"

"Frank," said Pancho. "*¿Y tú, cómo te llamas?*"

Just then someone needed to be blindfolded, and I missed the rest of their conversation. But as I tied the scarf across a small child's eyes and spun him round and round, I thought about the double lives these children all led: two names, two identities, two worlds. There in the dappled light of the pepper tree on a beautiful June afternoon, it was easy to forget about borders, about lines separating nations from their neighbors, children from their parents, doctors from their patients. It was easy to turn and turn under the piñata until all the lights and shadows merged, and all the faces blended, and laughter rained down from the shining leaves like bright-colored candy.

In late July, Cathy began talking about the party she wanted for her eleventh birthday in August.

"She's a real Leo," said my friend Marge, " born to party!"

We were sitting by Marge's pool, sipping vodka tonics and enjoying what I thought of as a "lost Saturday." Cathy and Josh were with their dad, and Carlos was spending the day with Charley. Afternoons like this were the best part of being single.

"But Marge," I wailed, "Cathy wants a piñata! Doesn't that seem strange to you? You're from New York; I thought you'd be on my side!"

"Wake up, girl, this is California," said Marge, slipping a Virginia Slim into a long black cigarette holder. "You should be thanking Quetzalcóatl that she doesn't want a goddamn male stripper."

I slugged back the last of my vodka tonic and headed into Marge's kitchen to mix another one. Marge was already on her third drink; her husband was at the Padres game and wasn't due back for hours. I continued talking through the screen door between the kitchen and patio.

"What the hell is happening to me and my family, Marge?" I asked rhetorically. "All those years of school, and here I am working at a clinic where they pay me with tamales half the time. I offer to take my daughter and her friends to lunch at the Sheraton for her birthday, and she'd rather have a piñata. And remember Josh and the *buñuelos*?"

Marge started snorting with laughter, puffs of smoke spurting from her nose. The previous December, Josh had come home from school one day announcing that he had to bring thirty *buñuelos*—sweet dessert tortillas—to class. When I questioned him further, he explained that the teacher wanted the American kids to bring Christmas cookies and the Mexican kids to bring *buñuelos*. Josh had just assumed he was a *buñuelo* kid.

"It's not funny, Marge," I said, setting my fresh drink on the patio table. "I think I'm messing up my kids' identities."

"You Aries chicks always want to control everything," Marge said. "Relax, will you please? Your kids are part of the new generation— Global Village and all that jazz. One World Family. Remember the '60s? And speaking of the '60s . . . "

She reached into a back pocket of her shorts and pulled out a small plastic bag and a slender pipe. "Wait till you try my latest harvest. I could never grow this stuff in New York . . . "

Cathy had her piñata, a big pink-and-yellow star filled with Hershey's Kisses and Tootsie Rolls and bags of gumdrops tied with gold ribbon. Six girls giggled and squealed while I blindfolded them in turn. Carlos, who was in charge of pulling the piñata up and down on its rope over the tree branch, let it dangle directly in front of the bat when it was Cathy's turn, and she smashed it with a satisfying thud. I shot Carlos a suspicious glance, but he was already busy setting up the volleyball net and deliberately avoided my eyes.

As I carried lemonade and birthday cake from the kitchen to the patio, I watched the girls running and laughing and rolling on the ground like so many kittens. Their T-shirts, now grass-stained and sweaty, clung damply to their budding chests, little bumps of incipient womanhood pushing through childish flesh. I stopped in the kitchen doorway to watch them, a stack of paper plates in my hand. They looked so innocent, so perfect. I wanted to stop the moment, freeze-frame their carefree beauty forever. A big tear rolled off my nose and plopped onto a paper plate.

"Oh, shit," I said hoarsely.

Carlos crossed the patio, took the plates from my hand, and put his arms around me.

"What's wrong?" he asked.

"This is the last time they'll ever be like this," I blubbered, hiding my face in his shoulder. "This is it, the end of their childhood. They look so free, so happy, but it's all over, it's all gone. Nothing will ever be the same again." I was sobbing by now, and I no longer knew if I wept for Cathy, for myself, or for the world around us as it turned inexorably away from innocence and into the shadowed future.

Nothing stays the same; everything changes. By 1982, Ronald Reagan is only halfway through his first term in office, but already the federal funds that have kept the clinic afloat have dried up and disappeared. By 1983, I am back at my old job with Children's Hospital. Cathy is a freshman in high school, and Charley, who has been living with his dad since 1981, is a junior. Josh is in his last year of elementary school. Jorge has bought three acres of land in the country and is living in a tiny trailer while he plants avocado trees and builds himself a little cinder-block house. Carlos has left the community college; he is working with Latino street kids as director of a storefront agency in the barrio. He and Charley live in a rented condominium, but spend most of their time with us.

The years have changed the border, as well. The barbed wire fence is more perforated than ever, and the clusters of men and women waiting there for nightfall stretch along its length for more than a mile. Vendors have appeared. Some wheel their carts up and down along the fence, selling tacos, sodas, hot dogs. Some have set up permanent stalls under bright blue plastic awnings where, besides food, they sell hats, blankets, and tapes. Lively ranchero music still rings with gay bravado from the Mexican side of the fence. But on the other side, in No Man's Land, bandits now lie in wait for easy prey. The border patrol has taken to buzzing the area with helicopters, and their green vans are now manned with reinforcements from Texas—officers who don't know the first names and family histories of their targets.

Everything changes, nothing stays the same. Sometimes, in those days, I felt as though I were running over the sand of a giant hourglass, and the faster I ran, the faster the sand slipped away beneath my feet.

I struggled especially during the so-called holiday season. I had never gotten used to facing holidays without the children, alternate Thanksgivings and Christmases, the price of joint custody. In December of odd-numbered years, I would find myself becoming insanely jealous of women with turkeys in their shopping carts, and I would become teary-eyed over Hallmark commercials on TV. So when Carlos proposed a trip to San Ignacio while our kids were gone in December of 1983, I agreed eagerly.

Bob and Sue wanted to join us, but Linda, now thirteen, balked at spending Christmas away from home. I had always admired Sue's sensible immunity to the Hallmark syndrome. She and Bob staunchly refused to surrender to the holiday hype; in fact, they usually tried to get out of town before it hit full force. Linda had spent more Christmases in Baja than she had at home, but now that she was an adolescent, she didn't want to miss the season's social events. A compromise was finally reached: Linda would spend Christmas at home with her grandmother and cousins and would be allowed to go to her friends' parties. Bob and Sue and Carlos and I would attend Christmas Eve mass at the old mission in San Ignacio.

In 1961, when the naturalist Joseph Wood Krutch visited San Ignacio, the only accommodations to be had were in the home of Señora Leree. When we arrived in 1983, Señora Leree was a distant memory, but two commercial establishments offered tourist lodgings. One was Hotel El Presidente, where we had passed a miserable night five years before. The other was the modest little Motel La Posada, owned by Oscar Fischer and his wife.

Staying at La Posada was very much like being a visitor in the Fischers' home. The motel office was the Fischers' dining table, and the six guest rooms were furnished haphazardly with old furniture from the house. In the small courtyard, guests mingled like instant family, sharing cheerfully: "Do you have an extra blanket in your room?" or "May I borrow your lightbulb for an hour?" The Fischers socialized with the guests, chatting amiably about the latest road conditions and the local gossip.

Carlos, who seemed to know everyone in Baja, was greeted warmly by Oscar with an embrace. While we were signing in at the dining-room table, Oscar went to a large carved wood cupboard from which he withdrew a yellow plastic pitcher, five small glasses, and a plate covered in a tea towel. In honor of Christmas Eve, he explained, he and his wife had been to the French bakery in Santa Rosalía that morning and had brought back *aguamiel* and French pastries. With a little flourish of pride, he filled each glass with a few ounces of the clear liquid from the pitcher, which I surreptitiously sniffed. It smelled clean and sweet, like the desert. Then Oscar lifted the tea towel and passed around the platter.

With the exception of two shriveled chocolate éclairs, the pastries looked exactly like Mexican *pan dulce*. There were three *conchas*, round spirals of sugary dough in the shape of conch shells, and two *orejas*, sweet breads named for the swirls and folds of an ear which they were said to resemble. But Santa Rosalía, a town created by a nineteenth century French mining company, commanded a certain grudging respect among the locals because of its European heritage; and, although the Santa Rosalía bakery produced exactly the same *conchas* and *orejas* as every other Mexican bakery, there seemed to be a general unspoken understanding that they were genuine French pastries, having been baked in the *panadería francesa*.

So we toasted Christmas Eve with *aguamiel*, the sweet syrup of the maguey cactus that becomes tequila when fermented—and we nibbled on Mexican-French pastries and éclairs. Oscar and Carlos caught up on their news.

"*La crisis económica*," Oscar said, shaking his head slowly. "It has been very bad." He raised his hat to run a hand through thinning blond hair. "Hard times," he said. "The government tells us we must tighten our belts. Every Mexican must help to pay off the country's debt, it is our duty to *la patria*. But we must eat, no?" Tourism had plummeted, he told us, while interest rates and the cost of tortillas had soared. Bank loans were virtually non-existent. He gestured toward an open window, indicating the empty lot across the street in which a concrete foundation had been poured.

"I was going to expand La Posada," he explained, "but my wife got sick, the medical bills . . . I had to abandon the project."

Carlos said, "One day things will be better, Oscar."

"*Dios quiera*," answered Oscar, "God willing." I thought of the boy I had met in the café in town five years before. He had answered me with the same words when I had told him that one day I would return to San Ignacio. "But meanwhile," Oscar went on, brightening up, "Tota's restaurant is better than ever. Tonight she cooks garlic shrimp for Christmas Eve. You must join us! "

"I remember Tota's shrimp," said Carlos, licking his lips. "We'll be there right after mass."

"Mass?" said Oscar, smiling at me. "You must have made a new man of that old sinner!"

I fingered the star of David I wore around my neck on a gold chain. I looked at Carlos for guidance. He reached across the table and took my hand.

"¿*Cómo no?*" he said. "She's *la doctora de mi corazón*, the doctor of my heart."

While Oscar and Carlos talked, I had been nursing my *aguamiel* and looking around the Fischers' dining room. In one corner stood a small artificial Christmas tree festooned with colored glass balls and little painted tin figures: a burro with a halo, a chipped red-and-green star. Under the tree lay a nativity scene, carved from wood and painted in pastel shades. The dining table at which we sat was covered in a clean white cloth embroidered with big red poinsettias. The Fischers' teenage son was helping his mother wind colored lights around a tall cactus in a clay pot by the door. Oscar, big-boned and fair, looked European, though his dusty boots and straw cowboy hat were pure Mexican. But his wife and son were both small and dark, their smooth, open faces as brown as San Ignacio dates.

Later, as Carlos and I strolled toward the plaza, he told me what he knew of Oscar Fischer's story. It was a story that had been repeated many times, with minor variations, throughout Baja, accounting for the many European surnames among the peninsula's inhabitants.

In the middle 1800s, copper was discovered about forty miles south of San Ignacio. A French mining company constructed the town of Santa Rosalía and built a port there from which, for many decades, European ships carried copper ore back to the Old World. Oscar's father had been a German sailor on one of those ships. During one of his stays in Santa Rosalía, he had fallen in love with a local girl and had slipped away with her to San Ignacio while his ship sailed off without him. In San Ignacio, he had put his German know-how to work, establishing a blacksmith and auto shop where he shod horses and repaired cars as the occasion demanded, and where he fashioned many of his own tools. Carlos had visited the shop in the late 1960s.

"The old man was amazing," he told me. "There was no electricity here, no technology at all. But he figured out a way to run his lathe. He had this old bicycle hanging from the ceiling of his shop, and he hired a kid to pedal it. The wheels of the bike turned the lathe."

"Wow," I said. "That's German ingenuity for you!"

"That's Mexican ingenuity," said Carlos. "He learned that here. Can you imagine a setup like that in Europe?"

"OK," I conceded, "it's a mixture of European technology and local resourcefulness. A hybrid. When you cross two breeds, you usually get a new organism with the best characteristics of each parent. In biology, we call that 'hybrid vigor.'"

Carlos shot me the look of mocking amusement he reserved for my more pompous moments.

"We invented hybrids hundreds of years before your scientists," he said. "In Mexico, we call them mestizos."

The plaza hadn't changed very much in the five years since I had passed through. The children who sold dates from baskets had been supplanted by a wooden stand at one end of the square on which dates were piled in little pyramids. A woman in blue knee socks sat in front of the stand on a wooden chair and stared impassively at the world, arms folded across a shapeless bosom. But the same Indian laurel trees still cast their deep shade over the same benches where the same old men sat gazing out at the afternoon. The café where I had sworn to return to San Ignacio still slumbered in the sunshine. And the old stone mission church, which had embraced the town for two centuries, still dominated the plaza like a benevolent matriarch. Its walls, once painted white, had reverted to their original earth shades, sand and brown. Above wide stone stairs worn smooth with use, magenta bougainvillea flanked carved doors of dark wood. Children ran up and down the stairs, in and out of the doors, crossing themselves automatically as they called to one another in high, excited tones.

Here in the center of town, the children's exuberance was the only reminder of the season. There were no tinsel garlands, no canned carols, no bell-ringing Santa Claus. There were only the old men and the children and the church, whose stone walls glowed with a warm gold light, the same glow that lit the distant hills where the sun was sinking down to Christmas.

Beyond the plaza, along a dirt-and-sand road that led eventually to the highway, a kind of heavy splendor enveloped San Ignacio in a spell. Surrounded on all sides by desolate desert, the arching date palms and deep green river seemed more dream than oasis, more fantasy than reality. Carlos and I stood on a little bridge over the river and watched big black crows rise lazily against a fiery sky. The air was moist, warm, sensuous, and smelled of water. Carlos put his arm around me and kissed the top of my head. "Merry Christmas," he said.

Having grown up with an ecumenical group of friends, I had been to many Christmas Eve services and had come to associate such events with twinkling lights, new clothes, stirring organ music. So I was surprised, and a little disappointed, when we pushed open the creaking wooden doors at a few minutes before 7:00 and entered a dimly lit, musty-smelling church where a few old women in black shawls sat scattered across the pews.

The interior was modest by the standards of European churches, but it must have seemed sumptuous to the Indians for whom the original mission was founded. The altar was richly carved and gilded, and the arched ceiling above it swarmed with faded saints, still smiling blissfully. Several alcoves along the wall flickered with the lights of votive candles. From one of the side walls, a carved golden cherub hung suspended, as if ready to take wing over the congregation. The cherub's high cheekbones and long, flat nose gave it a distinctly indigenous face. Just beyond this Indian angel stood a life-sized statue of Saint Ignatius himself. His wooden features were chipped and the paint faded, but his robe, white rayon woven with gold thread, looked new. From waist to ankle, the robe was covered with snapshots of children, pinned to the cloth. They stared out with wide, surprised eyes: a thin little girl with disheveled hair standing in front of a wooden shack; a baby in a christening gown, cradled between mother and father; a dark boy whose twisted body was supported on one crutch. One of the photographs looked like Esperanza, with the folded eyelids and innocent mouth of Down Syndrome. Above their trusting faces, San Ignacio raised his hand in endless blessing.

All this I saw from the corner of a pew where I shrank against the wall in an agony of self-consciousness. Not only did I feel disappointed and depressed by the modesty of this Christmas Eve scene, but I also felt painfully out of place. Before leaving home, I had carefully packed what I thought would be just the right holiday outfit: a green wool sheath with a strand of gold beads and a pair of green satin high-heeled pumps. Now, however, I felt like a gaudy metal Christmas tree in a forest of dignified pines. The Christmas Eve worshippers entered the sanctuary quietly, coming in directly from their day's activities as if they were simply stopping by a neighbor's house to visit on their way home. Many of the women clutched small bags containing the evening meal: a package of tortillas, or a slab of cheese. The men still wore their wide-brimmed straw hats, the sweat of the fields still drying on their necks. A woman with two little girls sat down beside me. The girls stared at me and giggled furtively. Their mother spoke to them firmly, then turned to me with a gentle, apologetic smile. I tried to smile back, but even my smile felt awkward. I had become separated from Carlos and Bob and Sue, who were a few rows behind me, and I fought down the urge to bolt.

By the time the priest stepped up to the altar, the church had filled up. Almost all the congregants were small and dark, but the priest was tall and blond with clear blue eyes and fair skin.

He was very young and very handsome, and I wondered if he had been banished to this remote outpost as a lesson in humility. But if he was being punished, he gave no indication of resentment; in his long white robes, his bearing was serene. Without ceremony or flourish, he began to read the beautiful words of the Christmas story. Even in Spanish, they sounded comfortingly familiar, and as I listened, I began to lose myself in the poetry.

I thought that Bethlehem must have been a lot like San Ignacio, a dusty little oasis in a desert land. I imagined Joseph leading his pregnant wife along narrow streets, and I thought that they must have looked a great deal like the men and women who sat in the wooden pews around me. Those men and women had gathered tonight, simply and naturally, to greet the newborn baby Jesus. There was no incense, no organ, no glittering holiday tinsel. With my extravagant and artificial expectations, I was as out of place here as Encarnación Mendoza had been among the antiseptic white coats of our clinic.

When the priest finished reading, he stepped down from the dais and stood at the front of the nave. With head bowed, he extended his arms to the people. In them he held—to my utter astonishment—a small, well-worn doll. It was a baby doll, such as a child might use, with plastic head and limbs and a cloth torso. The doll was unclothed and uncovered, and, for me, the sight was so incongruous that I almost laughed out loud. Whatever I had expected, whatever I had found, had not prepared me for the spectacle of a handsome young priest holding a shabby doll in his arms. But no one else seemed surprised at all. No word was spoken, no signal given; but suddenly the aisle was filled with congregants, all pressing forward toward the father. He simply stood there as if he had been carved from stone, a human altar whose only function was to hold out that tiny form to the people. They approached reverently, and each, in turn, bent and kissed the face of the doll, then turned and walked back down the aisle and out into the night.

Somehow, I found myself caught in the surging crowd and pushed toward the priest. My discomfort was rising toward panic; frantically, I looked around for an escape but found none. The heat of bodies pressing in and the smell of sweat and hair and breath made me feel faint. The saints seemed to whirl above me. Then I was there, and as I bent to kiss the Holy Child, my tears mingled with the salt of those who had gone before, and for a moment I thought that He smiled at me. Then I was out in the cool night air, stumbling down the smooth stone steps to the plaza. A young man with kind eyes caught my elbow to steady me. "*Feliz Navidad*," he said, and smiled.

Tota's restaurant was actually the patio of Tota's house. The patio, which had been enlarged and covered with a thatched roof, was attached to a small, enclosed kitchen. The main house stood across a courtyard where canaries twittered softly in a large wrought iron cage and cats crouched behind bushes of crimson hibiscus.

From the church plaza, we had picked our way along the cobble-stones of silent dark streets that seemed to lead nowhere. But when we finally rounded a corner into the rising hum of voices and the redo-lence of garlic, we knew we had found the spot. We entered through a wooden gate into a glow of candlelight and kerosene lanterns.

The little patio was jammed with tables and festive diners. From the far end, Oscar called out and waved us over to a long table piled with platters and surrounded by a crowd of chattering men and women. Somehow, four more chairs materialized for us. We shook hands with everyone amid animated introductions, and then we sat down to a Christmas Eve feast of shrimp dripping with garlic sauce along with mountains of beans, rice, and tortillas, all washed down with cold beer and laughter.

It was late when we finally got up to go, shaking hands all around. In the kitchen doorway, a large-boned woman sat on a straight-backed chair. Her arms were folded over a wilted white apron, and wisps of gray hair straggled from a bun at the back of her neck.

"Tota!" Carlos grasped both of her hands in his, and she looked up with a tired smile. "The shrimp were better than ever," he told her. "*¡Deliciosos!*"

"*Hechos con amor,*" she answered. "Made with love."

We awoke to the ringing silence of Christmas morning, the air hushed and vibrant like the aftermath of bells. Bob and Sue made coffee on their camp stove, which they set on a couple of concrete blocks in the courtyard of the motel. I brought out a tin of *biscotti* I had been saving for Christmas. We sat in the sun on wooden chairs collected from various rooms and watched dust motes float above Oscar's deferred dreams across the road.

Later we wandered down toward the center of town while, in the streets, children played with their new toys. A boy of about ten pulled a shiny red wagon in which two little girls sat rigid with delight, bounc-ing over cobblestones. In an empty lot, five boys darted through clouds of brown dust, chasing a bright white soccer ball that flashed among them like a beacon. In the plaza, a small boy in bright red shorts and a matching jacket pedaled a Big Wheel in widening concentric circles.

His stubby legs pumped furiously, and the plastic wheels spun noisy arcs of yellow across the gray stone stairs that led up to the mission. On one of its sweeps, the front wheel came within inches of colliding with an old woman in a black *rebozo* who, heedless of the hollow clamor, continued her slow, ancient ascent toward the open church doors above.

Bahía de Los Angeles

Cucurrucucu, paloma	Cucurrcucu, little dove
Cucurrucucu, no llores.	Cucurrcucu, don't cry.
Las piedras, jamás, paloma,	The stones will never know, little dove;
¿Qué van a saber de amores?	What will they know about love?

—Tomás Méndez, "Cucurrucucu Paloma"

In the autumn of 1984, the San Diego Padres won the National League championship for the first and only time in their history. By September, baseball fever had swept through the city. The stadium was packed, all the players were household names and local heroes, and everyone was bringing radios to work to listen to the games. As a season ticket holder, Carlos had two passes to the final playoffs against the Chicago Cubs who came to town on October 5, having won the first two games of the championship series at Wrigley Field.

On the morning of the first home playoff game, Carlos told me, "You can take Cathy and Josh to a game each, and I'll take Charley to the last game."

"How do you know there'll be three games?" I asked him. "We might lose tonight."

"There will be three games," he said. "Trust me."

He narrowed his eyes and folded the sports section of the newspaper, which he scrutinized while he sipped his coffee. I recognized the gesture as a sign that the discussion was over, and by the stern line of his mouth, I guessed that he had dreamed the future again.

Carlos hated to talk about his precognitive dreams, but I had come to respect them. One Sunday morning, two years earlier, he had awakened early, rolled over, and murmured sleepily, "I dreamed that your dad is trying to call you." A few hours later, my father telephoned from Philadelphia to let me know that my mother had died. Carlos never again mentioned his half-conscious comment, but I never forgot it.

So Cathy and I became part of the euphoric crowd that cheered the Padres to victory on October 5, and on the following night, Josh and I witnessed baseball history when Steve Garvey hit his bottom-of-the-ninth, over-the-fence, game-winning home run. Carlos and Charley went to the stadium for the final game, and Marge invited me and my kids to watch it at her house. Her husband Eddie was already glued to the TV when we arrived, and Cathy and Josh spread out on the floor beside him. Marge and I went out to her kitchen to make corned beef sandwiches.

"So what's new?" Marge asked, as we sliced rye bread.

"Well," I said, "I think I'm going to buy a VW van."

"What for? Carlos already has a van." She poured a Dos Equis beer into a chilled glass and passed it down the counter to me, then poured one for herself.

"Carlos's van is his," I retorted testily. "I want my own. Josh's piano teacher has a great 1968 van for sale."

"Jeez," said Marge, lighting a cigarette. "Why don't you and Carlos just do the deed already? You've known each other seven years, for crissake. His van's your van, you know what I mean? California's a community property state."

"Come on, Marge," I said, trying to make light of her comment. "How could I marry someone who's always late for everything?"

Marge said something that sounded like *D'ning d'nang narcoin, bu-bat, bu-d'lay*. It was one of her favorite phrases. She had learned it from the Montagnards, a mountain people in Viet Nam with whom she had worked as a nurse during the war. According to Marge, the rough translation was, "Today, tomorrow, next year. Who knows? Who cares?"

"I should have remembered not to bring up the subject of time with you," I said, grinning at her. Marge claimed that all watches stopped immediately upon contact with her wrist. "Carlos and I are just different, that's all." I drained my beer.

"Yeah," she said, "you're an Aries and he's a Pisces. So what?"

"Cut the astro-babble, Marge. You know what I mean. He's a Mexican."

"No shit, Sherlock," said Marge, refilling both our glasses. "Look," she said, stubbing out her cigarette. Her metallic blue eyes softened as she leaned across the counter toward me. In the dim light, they looked like gray pearls. "You two are crazy about each other. Everyone can see it. If you want my opinion, you're just chicken." She flapped her arms and made a clucking sound, then giggled. Her eyes crystallized back to blue.

"You're nuts, girl," I said fondly. I had to smile at her chicken imitation. "But think about this, Marge. Have you ever noticed that in Spanish, nobody's responsible for anything? It's a whole culture of fatalism, built right into the language. You don't miss the train, the train loses itself to you: *Se me perdió el tren.* If you drop a plate, it's actually the plate's fault: *Se me cayó el plato.* Can you imagine me living life as an indirect object?"

Marge started spreading Russian dressing on slices of rye bread, concentrating on the task. For a few minutes, the only sound was the clink of her knife going in and out of the jar. Then she said, quietly, "You're the smartest broad I know." She was waving the knife between jar and bread in long, sweeping strokes, as if she were wielding a magician's wand. "But for such a smart broad, sometimes you can be incredibly dense. Do you really believe you can be the subject of every goddamn sentence? Only Americans think they have that much control! Life is full of reflexive verbs and indirect objects. Shit happens. Karma happens. Love happens." She put the knife down, pushed a strand of sun-streaked hair off her forehead, and looked at me. "Life happens. Just let it in for once, Judy!"

I stared back at her. I could think of nothing to say. After a minute, she lit another cigarette and started piling corned beef on the bread.

"Well," I said dryly, "right now, I want to see what the Padres' karma is." I put the sandwiches on a tray and went into the den to watch the San Diego Padres become the National League champions.

The following week I sold my old Toyota station wagon to Jorge, whose property sprouted old cars like weeds, and I bought the Carters' van: a 1968 white pop-top VW with forty-five thousand miles.

Kay and Mark Carter had become good friends of mine when Josh took piano lessons from Kay, and the friendship persisted even after Josh quit practicing and gave up his lessons. Tara and Lisa Carter were the same ages as my kids, and we often got together for family picnics or afternoons at the beach. Mark Carter, a high school biology teacher, had fished the Sea of Cortés since the early '60s and considered it to be the closest place to Paradise that he had ever known. When I bought their van, they bought a brand new Toyota camper, and we began talking about taking a trip to Baja together.

Cathy and I sewed new curtains for the van out of white fabric, patterned with blue and burgundy flowers. "Girl curtains," Cathy called them. Charley helped Josh install a new tape deck and high-powered speakers. "Rad," Josh said when he slipped in his Bob Marley tape. And Carlos fine-tuned the engine, giving me a lesson in auto mechanics as he went along. Gradually I learned the gear patterns of the VW and became accustomed to using the right-hand side mirror rather than the rearview mirror when the back of the van was loaded with camping gear. Sitting high up and forward in the driver's seat, I felt like the captain of a ship. My sense of self-confidence grew with the miles.

In April Carlos decided to take Charley back to his hometown in Mexico for a visit during Charley's spring break. He wanted me to join them, but I had already planned a trip with the Carters to Bahía de Los Angeles on the Sea of Cortés. Mark claimed it had the best fishing in the world, and Kay said that the sunrises there made her cry.

Carlos came over to say good-bye the day before we were to leave on our respective journeys.

"I wish you were coming with us," Carlos said. "Everybody will miss you." I had met his mother several times during her visits to California, and I had met three of his aunts, two uncles, and various cousins when they came to see Disneyland.

"They won't miss me," I said. "They hardly know me."

"I can't believe you really mean that," said Carlos. His eyes darkened as they always did when he was angry or hurt. "They think of you as part of the extended family. The group's not the same without you."

"Well," I said shortly, "this isn't about group process. For me, this is about my own personal growth."

"Gringos," Carlos muttered, shaking his head."*¿Quién los puede entender?* Who can understand them?"

"Carlos, be logical." I was folding laundry on the kitchen table, smoothing out the wrinkles in one of Josh's T-shirts. "This trip to L.A. Bay has been planned since January. You just decided to go to Mexico last week."

"So change your plans," Carlos said. He put his hand over mine. "I'll take you to L.A. Bay at Christmastime."

I pulled my hand away and continued folding, carefully matching the creases in the legs of my khaki pants. "I don't want you to take me there, Carlos. I don't want anyone to take me anywhere. I've come to love Baja, and now I have to make it mine. I have to take myself there. I have to meet it on my own terms. Can you understand that?"

When I looked up at him, his eyes were like stones. "I don't know," he answered. "I'm trying to understand. I'm trying." He turned and went out the kitchen door without looking back.

"Carlos," I called, "say hello to everyone for me!" But he was already gone, pulling his van out of my driveway with the familiar rumble and clatter which I could now identify as spark plugs firing and pistons pumping. I savored my new-found knowledge, picturing the engine parts as if reviewing class notes for an exam.

Then, feeling my spirits sink as the sputter faded into silence, I remembered the first time I had dissected a human heart in medical school. Initially I had been fascinated by the intricate mechanics of valves and vessels and muscle. But when I had finished, and the heart lay picked apart on the metal dissecting table, I had experienced a sinking sensation like the one I was fighting now. *Is that all there is?* I had wondered. *Is that little piece of meat the same heart that swells with joy, breaks with grief, flutters with love? Do I really want this knowledge?* I was wiping my eyes with the back of my hand when Cathy and Josh came in, squabbling.

"Mom," Cathy wailed, "Josh wants to take my green sweatshirt

for fishing, but he'll get it all stinky! Tell him to take his own sweatshirt."
I went over to them and extended my arms, hugging them both at
once as I used to do when they were much smaller.

"Let's think of a name for the van," I said. "It's going to be our
home for a week."

Josh murmured, "Carlos says it looks like a big *paloma blanca* ."

"White Dove," Cathy translated. "That's a good name. Let's call
it *Paloma Blanca!*" *A good name*, I thought. *White Dove of luck, carry us
gently on our journey, whatever its destination might be.*

In the cold gray light of dawn the next day, with Cathy and Josh
dozing in the back, I steered Paloma Blanca out of the driveway and
followed the Carters' camper south. My mouth was dry and my heart
was racing, and I felt more alone than I could remember ever feeling
before. But by the time we stopped in Ensenada for gas and sweet
rolls, my initial anxiety had been replaced by an almost euphoric sense
of self-confidence: I had made it through the traffic in Tijuana without an incident, the engine was smooth and responsive to my touch,
the kids were excited, and the sun was sparkling over the Pacific. Kay
Carter rode with me from Ensenada to our next stop in Cataviña, and
Cathy and Josh rode with Tara and Lisa in the Toyota. By late afternoon we had turned off the main highway and were heading east over
a rough dirt road that carried us through the enchanted Baja desert
toward the Gulf.

Mexicans call it *el Mar de Cortés*, and U.S. maps label it the Gulf
of California. But on the old maps sketched with quill pens by early
Spanish explorers, it is called *el Mar Bermejo*, the Vermilion Sea. Some
have claimed that this name derives from the famous "red tides" which
sometimes fill the gulf with a myriad of tiny creatures that can turn
the ocean blood-red. But when I awoke to my first dawn over the Bay
of Angels, the rising sun was spreading vermilion fire across the sky
and the sea, and the mountains burned with gold-vermilion flames. I
knew then that the Vermilion Sea had been named by someone awak-
ening on just such a morning long ago to just such a sunrise over
Bahía de Los Angeles.

My only other experience of the Gulf coast of Baja had been on

Bahía Concepción, south of Mulegé. That seductive, tropical bay is like a lovely girl whose beauty glimmers through the soft veils and warm illusions of youth. But L.A. Bay's beauty is naked and fierce, like the fine-boned splendor of age. From the cold mineral blue of the sea, rise mountains as stark as truth, their jagged slopes uncompromised by vegetation. Deep-shadowed canyons hide fabled veins of silver and gold, still sought by madmen and dreamers from both sides of the border. And in a land of harsh exaggeration, L.A. Bay is the ultimate: Her tides are higher, her water colder, and her currents stronger than anywhere else in Baja. Perhaps because of these very conditions, the rich waters of this desert bay teem with marine life, and, like the grand old beauty that she is, *La Bahía* attracts admirers from all over the world: fishermen, biologists, divers, pilgrims.

The naturalist Joseph Wood Krutch was all of those. Of his visit to L.A. Bay in 1961 he wrote: "Why do they (and why did we) come? What are we looking for? . . . Thoreau said that many men went fishing all their lives without ever realizing that fish was not what they were really looking for. We come to see the world; and there is still a sizable minority who find the vanishing world dominated by nature rather than man one of the things most worth seeing . . . "

From the warmth of my sleeping bag cocoon, I watched the vermilion fire soften to bronze, then deepen to blue as the sun rose over the bay. The back door of the van was open to the salty air, and I could see Josh stirring in his sleeping bag on the sand below. Above me, in the canvas cot slung across the van's pop-top, Cathy snored softly. Along the shore, sandpipers hopped over wet stones, dipping their long bills for breakfast, while among them, looking like a large shore bird himself, Mark moved slowly across the beach, his fishing pole an extension of his arm against the brightening sea. Gulls bobbed lazily on the water, and a squadron of pelicans glided across the sky with long, slow wings. The sun crested the top of Guardian Angel Island, and suddenly the world was bathed in white gold. I slipped out of my sleeping bag and headed down to the shore.

When I reached him, Mark was crouched down on a rock, bent intently over something he held in his hand.

"Good morning," I called.

"Look at this little honey," he replied, without raising his head. I squatted down beside him. "The colors fade fast when you get 'em out of the water. But it's still fresh." The fish he held was switching its tail back and forth, and its scales shimmered like beaten copper in the morning sun. "Such delicate colors!" Mark was lost in wonder, absorbed by the beauty of the dying life in his hands. I could see why his students loved him.

"It's beautiful," I murmured.

Suddenly he bent his nose to the fish and inhaled deeply. "And so sweet!" he exclaimed. "That fishy odor is just an artifact of decay. Real fish smell great." He sat back on his haunches and extended the fish toward me, cradling it gently. "Smell."

I buried my nose in his cupped hands obediently. It was true: The fish was fragrant, salty, and fresh like the ocean. To my surprise, I was suddenly ravenously hungry.

"Yum!" I said. "I'm ready for breakfast!"

Mark grinned at me. "This is my breakfast," he said. "We're going to have to catch a few more of these to feed the family." He reached into the pocket of his shorts and pulled out a folded knife which he flicked open. Then he lay the fish on a rock and, with one smooth stroke, slit its belly from gill to tail. "Hmm," he mused, pulling a tubular organ from the fish's viscera. "Let's see what they're eating." With the tip of the knife, he pierced the stomach, then coaxed it open with his fingers. "Aha!" he exclaimed, holding up a macerated bit of flesh. "Sand crabs!" He couldn't have been more pleased had he found a nugget of gold. "Are the kids up? They can help me collect bait."

While Kay and I made coffee, the four youngsters scuttled along the wet sand, darting back now and then to Mark and his fishing pole. Their squeals and calls mingled with the calls of gulls, the squeals of sandpipers, and the hiss of tide on pebbles. They were wet and sandy when they came back up to camp, Mark the wettest and sandiest of all. But his bucket was full of fish, already gutted and cleaned. While Mark quick-fried breakfast over the camp stove, Cathy and Josh rinsed their hands in a bowl of fresh water on the table.

"We fed the guts to the seagulls," Josh told me nonchalantly. "They were all fighting over them!"

"It was so neat, Mom," Cathy said. "I never saw a fish's heart before." I smiled at her, musing. Where was the little girl who had been squeamish about eating lobster in El Rosario so many years ago?

The kids washed the dishes after breakfast while Kay and Mark and I sipped coffee and watched a *panga* heading for shore in the distance. Suddenly, to my right, I heard the clatter of a small rock slipping under a foot. When I turned to the sound, I almost dropped my coffee cup. Striding over the stones toward our camp was a Roman god: chiseled face under a crown of golden curls, muscular torso gleaming above thighs that I longed to touch. The thighs stopped a few feet from my face while I struggled to rise gracefully from my beach chair. I looked up into pale blue eyes and white teeth.

"*Buon giorno,*" said the god.

"Hi," said Kay.

Mark was on his feet. He was almost a head shorter than the young man, and more than twice his age, but somehow he made the god look like a big puppy dog.

"You spika Italiano?" asked the golden boy.

"Afraid not, son," said Mark. "I speak a little Spanish and pretty good English."

"I am Paolo," the youth said. "I see you pull many fish from the sea. What you use-a bait?"

Mark relaxed. "Sit down," he said. "You fish?"

I brought Paolo a cup of coffee, and he sprawled in Mark's beach chair while Mark tied knots in fishing line, cross-legged on the sand. Paolo was from Rome. He and his parents and younger sister had flown to Los Angeles, where they had rented a motor home and driven more than six hundred miles to this bay. They had come a long way to fish, but in their five days here their luck had been poor. Mark offered to take them out in his Zodiac, the little inflatable boat he had strapped to the roof of his camper.

"Bring your dad over," he told Paolo. "We need to go now, before the wind starts blowing."

Paolo bounded away and returned a few minutes later with an older version of himself, blond curls faded to gray and blue eyes framed in laugh lines. The father introduced himself as Giovanni Fulginetti and graced Kay and me with a melting smile before getting down to business. The three men wasted no time in small talk; the Zodiac was unloaded, inflated, and launched within twenty minutes. The motor sputtered a few times, then caught, and the little boat was soon just a yellow speck against the endless blue of the bay.

Cathy and Tara wandered down the beach collecting shells, while Josh and Lisa climbed over the rocks in search of tide pools. Kay and I played a couple of games of backgammon, and then I retreated into the van to read. The sun was hot, and the beach was still. I drifted into a hazy dream where Carlos's face smiled at me from beneath a crown of blond curls.

I awoke with a hammering heart: The van was shaking violently, and the whole world was moaning. Outside, our dishes, which the kids had stacked on the table, were scattered haphazardly across the sand. On the beach below, two dome tents rolled and bounced along the shore like tumbleweeds, chased by a couple of teenage boys. Kay was running after our chairs, which spun away just beyond her reach. Sand whipped my cheeks and stung my eyes.

"Where's the boat?" I yelled, but my voice was lost in the vastness of the wind. The four kids were standing by the water's edge, jumping up and down and waving. When I reached them, I saw that the ocean was the color of ripe plums. Whitecaps ripped across its surface, and little waves rolled frantically into shore as if trying to outrun the wind. I could see the yellow patch of boat far out across the wild bay. If it was moving at all, it was moving very slowly. There were no other boats in sight. Kay joined us, shading her eyes with one hand, brow furrowed.

"Pretty windy," she said. Kay was a no-nonsense woman, not given to overstatement. "Hope that little motor can make it."

"Bummer," said Josh. "It must be rad out there now! I wish I had gone."

"I'd be seasick for sure," Cathy said. "It makes me sick just to look out there."

"*Dad!*" yelled Lisa.

"He can't hear you, Lisa," Tara said scornfully. "Save your breath." Her young face was oddly pinched, her eyes mere slits as she squinted into the maelstrom. One arm was raised to hold a wide-brimmed hat on her head. With the other, she reached around her sister's shoulders and drew her close.

Kay muttered, "If they run out of gas, they'll blow all the way to Tiburón Island."

Isla Tiburón lies between the coasts of Baja California and Sonora and is the ancient home of the Seri Indians, reputed to be a fierce and bellicose band. But at the moment, the shrieking wind seemed a much more immediate threat than Indians. If the little boat ran out of gas, I doubted that it would last long enough to be blown to the island.

We stood there for what seemed like hours. Nothing happened. The patch of yellow didn't grow any larger, but it didn't disappear beneath the waves, either. The wind didn't abate. Kay never lowered her hand from her eyes, and Tara never lowered her arm from Lisa's shoulders. After a time we all grew bored with the crisis, since there was absolutely nothing any of us could do. There was no Coast Guard to call, and there were no telephones to call with. There were no lifeguards. There was not even a radio station to give a weather forecast, or a radio that could receive such a station. We were clearly the indirect objects of the wind's sentence. Whatever would happen would be utterly beyond our control, and my growing sense of fatalism brought a feeling of calm.

It was too windy to sit around outside, so we all huddled in the vehicles. The kids struck up a poker game. Kay and I read. I was flipping through the memoirs of Lieutenant Hardy, an officer in the British Royal Navy who had traveled in Baja during the 1820s. On one occasion, he had spent several days on Tiburón Island. Despite their reputation, none of the Seris had eaten him or shot him full of poison arrows. But when he had finally left the island, setting sail for more southern waters, a fierce gale had arisen out of nowhere and had blown his boat back to Tiburón. He described the Indians' knowing smiles when he staggered back onto their shore; the Seris seemed to believe that the storm was the product of their own powers. Lieutenant Hardy was convinced that they had deliberately employed those powers to force his return to them. I closed the book and stepped out of the van, squinting against the wind and gazing toward the water. The yellow boat was still there.

My curious sense of calm deepened; I seemed to have let go of some dark inner weight. In the place where that burden had been, I now discovered a kind of lightness and peace that was entirely new to me. Across that bright inner space floated a phrase like an aerial banner against a summer sky. It was a phrase that formed itself in Spanish, unbidden by my conscious mind. "*Se te fue el miedo,*" the banner said, naming me as the indirect object. "The fear has gone from you."

In time, the wind stopped, and the boat came *putt-putting* in to shore. Paolo jumped out, eyes blazing and cheeks flushed, exclaiming in rapid Italian. Giovanni and Mark pulled the boat onto the sand and lifted out a bucket overflowing with fish. All three men were dripping wet and shivering, and Mark looked pale. They had, in fact, been stranded, unable to make any headway against the gale and forced to simply wait it out. Paolo was beside himself with excitement.

"It was very, very . . . how you say? It was cool, baby!"

"Cold is what is was," said Giovanni, in excellent English. "Come on, Paolo, your mother will be worried." Kay and the children and I had come down to welcome the sailors home, and Giovanni turned to us. "Your husband is a master fisherman," he said to Kay. "Please join us at our camp for dinner tonight. We'll have a seafood banquet!"

When we crested the sandy rise between our camp and that of the Fulginetti family, we could see the glow from their campfire bathing them all in the soft light of an Italian Renaissance painting. They were leaning toward the warmth, enclosed in a bright cameo against the night. We greeted each other with a flurry of handshakes and cheek-pecks, and we all sat down on rocks or logs or beach chairs around the hearth. Signora Fulginetti wore an old pair of red sweatpants and an oversized white blouse knotted at the waist. Her thick dark hair was swept off her face with a silk scarf of wide red and blue stripes, and the total effect was pure elegance. I tugged at my dusty gray sweatshirt and tried to smooth my unruly mane, but gave it up as futile. Paolo's twelve-year-old sister, dressed in a Mickey Mouse T-shirt and torn Levis, could have passed for an American except for a kind of casual grace that she exuded like fine perfume. Paolo and Giovanni still wore their daytime attire of shorts and muscle shirts, but their sculpted bodies looked even more godlike in the firelight.

We feasted on fish and, of course, on pasta, and washed it all down with copious draughts of red wine served in tin cups. Kay and I chatted with the *signora*, she speaking in Italian and we in Spanish. We understood each other perfectly, and the conversation ranged from the preparation of marinara sauce to the challenges of life as a working wife and mother. Josh tried out his Spanish on the young *signorina* who rewarded him with radiant smiles, and the three girls worshipped at Paolo's feet while he described, in incomprehensible English, the family's adventures in Baja. Mark and Giovanni talked fishing, and Mark, after a few cups of wine, shared with Giovanni the Mark Carter Fishing Rules, developed and refined over decades of experience.

"First," he drawled, "fish where there are fish." Giovanni looked at him curiously. "I don't know about in Italy," Mark said, "but you'd be surprised how many suckers drop their lines into rivers that haven't seen a fish in years." Giovanni chuckled. "Rule number two," Mark went on, "fish when the fish are hungry. And finally . . . " He paused. Mark was a great storyteller, sensing when he had his audience enthralled. "Finally," he repeated, "when the fish talk to you, listen!"

The fire had burned down, and a bright half-moon flew over the hulk of Guardian Angel Island like a sail on the mast of a ghost ship. Nets of silver floated across the dark, quiet sea. The air was filled with a great hush, and it was time to sleep.

As we were taking our leave, Mark asked Giovanni, "You could have gone anywhere to fish. Why did you come all the way from Rome to this lost place?"

Giovanni stood by the fire's dying embers and extended his arms wide, as if to embrace the night. He threw back his head and smiled up at the stars. Then he dropped onto his haunches and gazed into the glowing coals. "There is no place left in Europe where the world is still as God created it," he said, softly. "The Old World has not understood man's relationship to nature. Only here is there still a chance."

Then he rose, and we all said goodnight. As we crested the little sandy hill, I looked back. The family was still standing where we had left them, pale shapes in the moonlight, huddled close together against the encroaching dark.

The first European to explore Bahía de Los Angeles was a Jesuit missionary who, in 1746, found a small band of indigenous families living along its beaches and fishing its fertile waters. Those waters have continued to yield up their bounty for generations of fishermen. Until the 1970s, L.A. Bay was particularly known for its abundant turtles, and Mama Díaz's fried turtle steaks were famous among the American fishermen who, landing their small craft at the primitive airfield, could always find a bed and a meal at the Casa Díaz.

But by the time we arrived, the *tortugas* were almost extinct, and the Mexican government had outlawed their capture except for conservation purposes. In the days following our dinner with the Fulginetti family, I thought about the disappearance of those marvelous creatures, and about Giovanni's long journey from Europe in search of unspoiled nature.

It was true that the bay was still rich in marine life. Snorkeling around the rocky points, we encountered gardens of scarlet and yellow sponges, shimmering walls of schooling jack, quick little angelfish like darting rainbows among the rocks and hollows. Once, we surprised a purple octopus in a crevice, and it shot away in a cloud of ink. Mark was a salty pied piper, leading us on single-file expeditions through the shallow water along the shore. He showed us how to shuffle the sand to avoid treading on the sting rays that often rose before us from the ocean floor like prehistoric birds, their great wings beating an ancient rhythm. The children found tiny clam shells, rosy with the colors of dawn, and polished cowries and carved sand dollars. But none of us ever saw the green and graceful shadow of a sea turtle, and I couldn't help mourning their absence and wondering what species would be the next to go. Although I had no doubt that Guardian Angel Island did somehow protect these waters with enchanted wings, it still seemed too fragile an ocean, too vulnerable a paradise, to meet Giovanni's hopes for much longer.

Perhaps it was these melancholy thoughts that began to weigh me down. Or perhaps it was the land itself. By noon every day, the heat lay over me like a leaden cape, and any movement or even any thought seemed like too much effort. There was no shade. The plastic canopy we put up every morning blew down in the relentless wind every afternoon. The colors were too intense, sea and sky like the facets of a sapphire with the bronze mountains etched into its edges. My eyes ached with so much light, and the wind exhausted me. I grew weary of fish and birds and reptiles, and I longed for the company of other mammals: a nice fuzzy cow, or a sad-eyed burro, or even a goat. At night, the stars hung unblinking in a black sky, as cold and silent as stones.

At last, it was time to head out. We broke camp and packed up the vehicles in the gentle morning light, before the curtain of heat came down and before the wind could strike. My last glimpse of the Bay of Angels was through the van's side mirror as we bounced over the rough dirt road toward the highway. The Gulf sparkled like blue satin under the late morning sun. A pelican dove for a fish, and a frigate bird circled effortlessly over the swells. The mountains glowed rose and copper and gold against a cobalt sky. The beach stretched away into the white distance, blank as a bone.

My spirits improved considerably as we approached the enchanted desert gardens of Cataviña. Boojum trees, some of them fifty feet tall, danced against a perfect sky. Huge granite boulders lay scattered across the land like dozing giants.

I had always been curious about the origin of those boulders, found only in the Cataviña region; and about why the boojum trees grow nowhere else on earth. Mark spoke convincingly of tectonic plates and ancient volcanic eruptions, of winds and waters of countless millennia, and of specialized seeds deep in the earth. It sounded good, but secretly I thought about the shamans of the ancient races who had vanished from these lands. Legend had it that they had been giants, come down from another world; perhaps the boulders and the boojums were their spirits, still guarding their ancestral home.

When we stopped for lunch under one of the blue palms growing by Cataviña's mysterious desert springs, everyone could feel the special energy of the place. An almost palpable vibration emanated from the sand and shimmered in the air. A blue butterfly floated beneath a mesquite. A lizard scampered onto our picnic blanket, then froze in terror when he realized what he'd done. Josh almost caught him. The girls wandered off to look for more butterflies. Kay and Mark took turns peering through a pair of field glasses, searching for a bird—a vermilion flycatcher—reputed to live by the spring. I dozed.

Later, we all took a walk through the palm-lined arroyo that led up toward Rancho Santa Inés, and finally we decided to go back to the vehicles and drive to the ranch to see if Doña Josefina might be around. It had been more than six years since I had first looked for her, and she had been away on that occasion. I had forgotten about her reputation as a woman of special power until now, and a little thrill of anticipation ran up my spine. *Still*, I thought, *I've come a long way since that first trip*. Then I had been a wide-eyed, credulous youth of thirty-five, shepherding two little kids; now I was a seasoned, independent woman whose children were more than half grown. Unconsciously, I squared my shoulders as I maneuvered my van onto the paved area beside Doña Josefina's hacienda.

But when the young man in the kitchen said that the *señora* was in, I froze like the lizard who had wandered by mistake onto our blanket. If I could have scuttled away like he had, I would have done so. But it was too late; the famous *bruja* was on her way to greet us.

She emerged from the old adobe house, a small woman of almost eighty years, round body neat and elegant in a simple black dress adorned with a strand of pearls, raven hair pulled back in a bun at the neck in the old Spanish style. Her skin was remarkably white and soft for someone who had spent a lifetime in the desert. Dark, piercing eyes gleamed with intelligence, and her smile was as sweet and pink as melon.

Mark and Kay and I introduced ourselves, and Doña Josefina greeted us warmly, with genuine interest. The children came over, and somehow she had them all on her lap before I could see how it happened. Josh had not sat on my lap for at least five years, and Cathy, who was fifteen, only did so in jest. But all four kids seemed to sink into her folds like butterflies settling into a flower, and she murmured over them softly while a little breeze moved the leaves of the palo verde tree above her. Then she looked directly at me.

"You are alone?" she asked. Her English was almost perfect, but for a moment I didn't understand what she meant. Her eyes held mine; their steady gleam made me think of those cold stars in the night sky of Bahía de Los Angeles.

"Yes," I answered. "*Sí, señora. Estoy sola.*"

There was no more than that to the interchange. Doña Josefina invited us to stay, and she supervised the preparation of her famous enchiladas for our supper. She was cordial and gentle and hospitable. But that night I dreamed that I was lying on a table in the desert, my feet up in stirrups, giving birth. Only the thing that emerged from my womb was not a human baby, but a hideous monster, black and twisted, as though it had been burned in a sacrificial fire. And the midwife attending the birth was Doña Josefina herself, who appeared as a giant silhouette against the night sky, dancing a wild dance beneath the indifferent stars.

We pulled into our own driveway the following evening, and I half hoped to find Carlos and Charley waiting there for us. But the house was dark and empty, echoing coldly when we went in.

The next morning, however, while I was making *huevos rancheros* for breakfast, my ears caught the faint sound of a Volkswagen engine. I stopped, spatula in midair, and listened; and as the familiar clatter drew closer, I felt my heart swell a little and dance in my breast like the fluttering wings of a dove.

San José del Cabo

... *Y por eso los grandes amores* *de muchos colores me gustan a mí*...	... And that's why the great and many-colored loves are the ones for me...

—Traditional song of the United Farmworkers' Union, "De Colores"

When Charley graduated from high school, Carlos and Jorge celebrated the event with a traditional Mexican fiesta at Jorge's ranch. Over the years, Jorge's three acres had blossomed with scores of avocado and citrus trees, and his original cinderblock hut had sprawled into a rambling three-bedroom ranch house. Behind the house and overlooking the grove stood an an old California oak tree, and in its shade, Jorge had constructed a rough wooden picnic table where, on warm afternoons, he and his workers gathered to share a meal and take a rest from the unending chores of Rancho Rodríguez. It was near this tree that he and Carlos planned to dig a deep pit in which to cook the *birria* for the fiesta.

A week before Charley's party, Carlos and I drove over the rutted dirt road to Jorge's property for a planning session. It was 1:00 in the afternoon, and the men were just coming up the hill for dinner. Jorge's sister, who was visiting from Tecate, greeted us warmly and set two more plates on the picnic table.

"*¿Cómo está el chivo?*" Carlos inquired, helping himself to a cold beer from the cooler under the oak. "How's the goat?"

Jorge wiped the sweat from his brow with a grimy red handkerchief. He was building a stone retaining wall behind his house and was covered in dust.

"The goat is growing fatter every day," he grinned. "He will make perfect *birria* by next week! *¿Verdad, Chuey?*" He handed his handkerchief to a stocky middle-aged man whose adobe-colored face was also streaked with dust. The two sat down at the table together, and Chuey smiled shyly.

"*Sí, profesor,*" he answered. "*Es verdad.*"

Chuey had been working for Jorge since they had planted the first seedlings in the hard, bare earth. He had become more a friend than a worker and had proven himself so skilled in so many areas that Jorge called him *maestro* and Carlos referred to him respectfully as Don Chuey. He could build a rock wall without mortar, fitting the stones together with patient precision, turning each stone over in his hands until he discovered the right shape, the complementary facet. He could find the level measure of a wall or a foundation with nothing more than a length of broken hose, filling it with water and adjusting it until no liquid spilled out either end. He had scattered chamomile seeds on the dry, packed dirt in front of Jorge's house where not even weeds had grown, and now the air was fragrant with hundreds of little yellow blossoms.

Chuey's father had been a *curandero* in Chihuahua, and Chuey often brewed herbal teas for the various ills of the men who congregated around Jorge's table. Although I was genuinely interested in folk remedies and the medicinal use of plants, I had been unable to break through the shy silence in which Chuey cloaked himself whenever I approached him. We had known each other for three years, and he had said little more to me than "*Buenos días, doctora.*" Then one afternoon, without warning or explanation, he had presented me with the *hongo chino,* a large, black, malodorous mushroom in a Ziplock baggie which Chuey handled with the tenderness of a father cradling his baby. He had appeared unannounced at my back door while I was cooking dinner.

"I saw the Chinese doctor yesterday," he said, when I invited him in. I was so surprised by his visit and by the full sentence he had spoken to me that I didn't think to ask who or what the Chinese doctor was. "He gave me this mushroom," Chuey continued, "and a recipe for making a tea. A very powerful tea." He pulled from his back pocket a crumpled scrap of notebook paper on which he had written the Chinese doctor's recipe. We both sat down at my kitchen table, and he placed the plastic mushroom bag and the scrap of paper in front of me. "It's important to follow these instructions exactly," he said. He kept his eyes lowered, avoiding my gaze. "If you change them in any way, the tea will be like poison."

I was silent a moment, reading the recipe. It involved multiple steps and required three days to complete. I felt honored and bewildered by Chuey's trust in me, and overwhelmed by the responsibility it implied. "What is the tea for, Chuey?" I asked.

"When the tea is prepared," he answered, "it should be perfectly clear, like water. If it is made correctly, it will bring you great energy." Finally he looked at me, and his eyes, deep in his lined face, glowed like green-gold moons. He smiled gently. "I will come back in three days," he said. "We will try the tea together."

It was my turn to look away. "Thank you, Chuey," I murmured. "I'll do my best."

As the recipe demanded, I went out and bought a new pot that had never known a drop of animal fat or other non-herbal substance. I found myself handling the mushroom with a kind of reverent awe, half expecting it to metamorphose before my eyes into some monstrous woman-eating fungus. Faithfully I soaked it and rinsed it and boiled it and rinsed it again, and soaked it under the midday sun and covered it against the moonlight. The mushroom seemed to undulate and breathe in the depths of the black pot, and a strange sediment swam the in the dark water.

On the morning of the third day, I lifted the lid with trembling fingers and peered into the pot. The amber liquid was translucent and as sparkling as a tropical topaz, and the mushroom had become a small white button like a benign little seed on the bottom of the pot. I gasped involuntarily, and whispered, to no one, "I think it worked!" When Chuey showed up later, he strode into my kitchen with a new familiarity. Without a word, I brought him the large glass jug into which I had poured the tea. He held it up against the sunlit window, inspecting it through narrowed lids. Then he set it down on the counter and turned to me with a slow smile.

"My own mother couldn't have done any better," he said. It was one of the greatest compliments I had ever received.

Chuey and I shared the tea, and I imagined that I felt a surge of extraordinary energy. But, more importantly, I seemed to have passed some kind of test. The Chinese mushroom episode had created a bond of mutual respect and affection between Chuey and me, and ever since then he had been much more relaxed in my presence. Now, under Jorge's oak tree, he passed me a plate of steaming tortillas while he briefed me on the condition of the men who were eating and chatting and laughing around the long table.

Darío, who didn't know exactly how old he was but who couldn't have been more than nineteen, had broken his right arm in Mexico and had never received any medical attention. The bone had healed without ever being properly aligned, so that his arm was sharply angled between elbow and wrist, and he was unable to fully rotate his right hand. Despite this minor handicap, Darío was a tireless and uncomplaining worker, strong as a yearling stallion and full of the same bounding energy. I knew that his arm would give him more trouble in the future and that he had a good chance of developing painful arthritis by the time he was Chuey's age. But the only cure I knew was surgery, and the boy could not afford an operation on either side of the border. Chuey had made a paste from aloe vera, which he rubbed on the deformity. Darío submitted to the treatment with the same cheerful patience with which he toiled in the avocado grove or hauled rocks up the hill to the wall.

Toño and Gilberto were brothers in their mid-twenties. They both had the slight build and burnished copper complexion of their native Guerrero, with the smooth beardless cheeks of their Indian ancestors. Toño went about his labors with a somber air, silent and morose, plodding up and down the hill with the heavy tread of a weary mule. Gilberto, whose dark brown eyes were flecked with little golden lights, moved like a colt, never walking when he could run, never running when he could prance. It was Gilberto's voice that floated up the canyon on Saturday nights, entertaining the workers' camp with songs of home—sung to the tinny strains of an old cracked guitar. And it was Gilberto who was Chuey's biggest concern that afternoon.

"He has been coughing for many weeks," Chuey confided to me. "I give him lemon grass tea and *yerba santa,* but he doesn't get better."

"Is he losing weight?" I asked.

"Possibly." Chuey glanced down the table at Gilberto, who was chattering to Toño. Toño was grinning uncharacteristically; only Gilberto could make him smile. "Yes, I think he looks thinner," said Chuey gravely.

Could be tuberculosis, I thought. To Chuey I said, "I'll bring a tuberculosis test with me next time I come over. Maybe he needs some medicine."

"*Primero, Dios,*" answered Chuey, and reached for another tortilla.

Charley's party was a big success. On Friday morning, Toño and Gilberto dug a deep pit while Chuey dispatched the goat's spirit to its Maker. Carlos and Jorge cut young maguey leaves from the plants that grew wild on the ranch. The goat meat, cleaned and chopped, was wrapped lovingly in the leaves. Darío brought armloads of dry oak wood to the pit, and Chuey lined the sides of the pit with stones. Then everyone had lunch while the oak fire burned down to embers. After lunch, Chuey laid the leaf-wrapped bundles in the earthen oven, and Darío filled the pit, covering the embers and the goat meat bundles with dirt. By 3:00 on Saturday afternoon, when the meal was brought out and served to the assembled guests, it had been transformed into *birria:* a sweet and tender stew that melted like butter in the mouth.

"This goat died a glorious death," Jorge declared, wiping the juice from his chin. "We are appreciating its essence!" The *birria* was accompanied by a strolling trio of musicians, friends of Carlos and Jorge from the college where they had taught. The afternoon rang with rousing Mexican music until even the teenagers were dancing. Later, Charley brought out his CD player and slipped in some American rock, and Carlos and I spun around the patio along with the youngsters to the music of Van Halen.

On Monday, when I went to work, I was still humming "*Volver, Volver,*" and I walked down the hospital corridor to my 8:00 meeting with a light tread. The meeting room was full. The Child Abuse Consultation Committee consisted of hospital social workers, child therapists, and pediatricians from both the hospital and the community. We met monthly in order to provide peer support in a difficult field and to share input on some of our more complex cases.

Cindy, one of the social workers, opened the Monday meeting with a case that had come to light three weeks before. An eight-year-old girl had been accosted and sexually molested on her way to school. The suspect was a Mexican male who had been apprehended a few hours after the incident. He was in police custody, and the girl was in counseling; there were no real glitches in the case. The only reason she was bringing the case up, Cindy explained, was to make us aware of the special flyers that the school district officials had sent out to all parents. Cindy passed a stack of these flyers around the conference table. I read the brief message, neatly printed on school district letterhead. I shook my head in disbelief and read it again.

Dear Parents,

We are all aware of the recent influx of Mexicans into our community. Because of the rise in the crime rate associated with these demographic changes, we are recommending that those of you with children who walk to and from school arrange for your child to be escorted by an adult. We cannot provide security for our students when they are off the school grounds. It is up to every one of us to increase our vigilance in these challenging times.

I looked up, face burning, and scanned the table for signs of outrage. People were sipping coffee from styrofoam cups, doodling in the margins of the flyers, checking pocket calendars. No one seemed at all distressed, but I found that I was trembling uncontrollably. I took a deep breath to steady myself, and I deliberately kept my voice low.

"This is the most racist thing I've ever seen," I said, as calmly as I could. A dozen pairs of eyes turned to me. Most of them showed mild surprise. Some of them were simply blank.

"What do you mean?" Chad was a colleague of mine, another of Children's Hospital's staff pediatricians.

"Well," I sputtered, "I mean . . . I mean . . . How dare they assume that more Mexicans mean more crime? That's just pure racism!"

The looks of mild surprise shifted to looks of incredulity. One of the therapists spoke up, and her conciliatory tone irritated me beyond reason.

"I can see that you're upset," she began. *Don't you use that psycho-babble on me!* I wanted to scream. She continued serenely. "But I don't think there are any assumptions being made here. Everyone knows that the local crime rate rises wherever there's an increase in the Mexican population."

I had a sudden flashback. A few weeks before, as I was parking my car at the supermarket, I had noticed a commotion in front of the store. A small dark man in shabby clothes was running desperately from the entrance, pursued by three burly guards who were all shouting and grabbing for their holsters. As the criminal fled, he clutched his precious loot to his chest: one loaf of Wonder Bread.

All I could say now was, "Everyone doesn't know that." My voice was breaking despite my efforts to control it. "I don't know that." I closed my eyes against the tears that threatened to spill over, and I could see Darío with his crooked grin and crooked arm. I could see Gilberto dancing, and I could see the sweet serious face of Toño. I could see Chuey's luminous eyes. Summoning all my rapidly-fading powers of logic, I opened my eyes and took a deep breath. "Look," I said, "we get thousands of child abuse reports every year. How many of the perpetrators are Mexican? If you check the numbers you'll see that they're no different than any other group."

Cindy looked annoyed. "I didn't mean for this to be a big deal," she grumbled. "It was informational only. I'm sure no one here is a racist."

That night at the dinner table, I told Carlos about the meeting. He shook his head grimly, eyes hard.

"The turkeys," he said. Then he recounted an episode from his own experience. One day, driving from Tijuana into San Diego, he had been detained by a surly border guard who had refused to believe that Carlos was a U.S. citizen. Finally, the guard had demanded to see Carlos's citizenship papers. With undisguised sarcasm, Carlos had retorted, "I don't carry my citizenship papers with me. Do you?"

"Oh, Carlos," Cathy breathed. Her round blue eyes filled with tears. "You could have been arrested!"

"*Pinches cabrones*," muttered Carlos. Then he winked across the table at Josh, who had known for years how to swear in Spanish. Josh winked back with an exaggerated grimace and passed Carlos the bowl of beans.

Later, in bed, I began to cry. Carlos held me close.

"Mirasol," he whispered, "now you're really *mexicana*. Don't let them get you down. You have to believe on yourself."

"In," I sniffed. "Believe in, not believe on. You always get that wrong."

"Thanks, Teacher," Carlos chuckled. "I guess you're still part gringa, after all."

For a long time, we lay quietly, savoring each other's warmth. Then Carlos murmured, "Let's get the hell out of here."

I pulled back and looked at him, puzzled. He raised himself on one elbow and gazed past the top of my head.

"A guy I work with is a surfer," he said. "He's rented a little shack down near San José del Cabo for the month of August, but he wants to sublet it for a few days. Let's go down there, just the two of us. We'll forget about all this *mierda;* you can count in it."

"On, not in," I smiled, pulling him gently down to me. "You can count *on* it."

The Mexican journalist Fernando Jordán conceived of the Baja peninsula as a thousand-mile-long arm embracing the mainland. The Los Cabos region, then, would be the sensitive fingertip at the end of that arm, endlessly stirring together the waters of the Pacific Ocean and the Sea of Cortés where they meet at Land's End. And encircling this fingertip like a golden ring, the Tropic of Cancer sets off the final fifty miles of the peninsula as the true tropics, a region once known as *la tierra perfumada,* the perfumed land.

Los Cabos, the tropical region that lies between Santiago and Todos Santos to the north and San José and San Lucas to the south, has been spinning its sweet, seductive web through almost three centuries of discovery. Its history abounds with stories of love and stories of death, and all the stories mingle in the soft green mist that lies over the land like a dream.

First, there were the pirates. During the late seventeenth and early eighteenth centuries, English privateers plied the turquoise seas of southern Baja, waiting for the treasure-laden Spanish galleons that rested in the harbors of Loreto, La Paz, and San José del Cabo. Some claim that the men were bewitched by the fields of *damiana*, that fragrant native flower said to be a powerful aphrodisiac. Others claim that it was the natural charms of the local women, warm and yielding as the tropical earth. But whatever the magic, many of the young English sailors on those pirate ships found treasure more precious than Spanish gold, and they never returned to England, preferring instead the hearts and hearths of the *tierra perfumada*. They, and the whalers who followed them two centuries later, brought with their love the seeds of death, for the native races were decimated by European diseases. But still, in the fields and villages of Los Cabos, the mestizo ranchers and fishermen bear their names: Heart and Collins, Smith and Green.

Then there were the padres. When Father Tamaral arrived in 1730 at San José del Cabo, he found a band of Pericú Indians living a life of sensual indolence in their earthly paradise there at the end of the world. To the good Jesuit father, the polygamous Pericúes were sinners, and he labored tirelessly to bring to them the word of his god and the dubious blessings of matrimony. But in 1734, the natives rose up against the Jesuits and their foreign religion: The priest in Santiago was killed and his church burned, and Father Tamaral was beheaded in front of the mission at San José del Cabo. Although his church survived the Pericú revolt, it was destroyed in 1918 by a great *chubasco*, one of the tropical hurricanes that periodically roars in from the sea wreaking vengeance on natives and foreigners alike.

Today, nothing remains of the cape's missions, nor of the Indian people by whose sweat they were built. However, the padres' legacy lives on—in the fields of sugar cane, the mango groves, the fig trees, and the date palms that still bless the land with abundance. But perhaps the Pericúes have had the last laugh after all, for in Cabo San Lucas, now a major international resort, hedonism has been resurrected as the true religion. In the shade of palm trees by tropical watering-holes, indolent tourists lie about enjoying the sensual pleasures of that sensual land, as did the ancient Pericúes, to the despair of the ancient Jesuit padres.

On a Wednesday morning in late August, we boarded an Aeroméxico plane in Tijuana, bound for the new airport outside of San José del Cabo. During the ninety-minute flight, I read the memoirs of Arthur North, an American adventurer who had traveled through Baja by foot and by burro during the first decade of this century.

"Listen to this," I said to Carlos. He was snoring, his head leaning against the window, but I read aloud anyway. " 'It is a frequent saying down the Peninsula that if a man stops a week at San José del Cabo he becomes a lotus eater and only ropes can haul him away.' "

"Good thing we're only staying for five days," murmured Carlos without opening his eyes. We couldn't have have known then that we would not escape so easily.

At the airport, we rented a VW bug. As Carlos eased the car onto the highway, I read the scrawled directions for finding the surfer shack.

"About five miles south of the airport," I read, "there are four palm trees growing close together on the left-hand side of the road. Go past them for a few yards until you see the jacaranda. Turn onto the dirt road by the jacaranda and double back behind the palm trees. The house is hard to see, so look for the black dog. She'll lead you home."

"That must be Señora," Carlos said. "Jim said she's the house dog. All the surfers know her."

"Let's hope she's expecting us," I commented dryly. "Otherwise, we'll be driving around palm trees all day."

I needn't have worried. The four palm trees were waving gently, as if in greeting, and the bright orange jacaranda blossoms—unique to the tropics—seemed to light up the little dirt path. As we turned, a skinny black dog walked slowly out of the overgrown brush by the roadside and stood directly in front of the car, looking up at us with clear, intelligent eyes. Although she stood about two feet high at the shoulder, her full teats almost brushed the ground. Satisfied that she had spotted her new people, Señora turned and trotted up the road. She stopped in front of a tall poinsettia bush and wagged her tail expectantly. We were home.

Hidden behind the poinsettia and its surrounding tangle of vines was a small structure with an overhanging roof of palm leaves. Carlos ran his hand across the ledge above the front door and found the key.

"Just where Jim said it would be," he observed, and we went in.

The door led into an enclosed entryway. Immediately to the right was a large kitchen with open shelves covering plywood walls. Beyond the kitchen was a tiny bathroom with a toilet and sink. Directly ahead was the main living area, a large *palapa* open on three sides. One back wall and three smooth poles supported a broad, sloping roof of palm thatch over a concrete floor. A warm breeze blew in from the sea, and the surf boomed softly just fifty yards away. At the far end of the living area, a cotton sheet in wavy patterns of green and blue hung from the roof, curtaining off the bedroom behind it: three concrete walls, from one of which extended a concrete platform covered with a mattress and bedding. In the middle of the *palapa* stood two Mexican leather chairs facing the beach; the only other furniture was a small wooden table and two rickety chairs in the kitchen.

I put down my bag by one of the leather chairs. I wasn't sure whether to feel enchanted or dismayed by the simplicity of the place. In truth, my feelings at that moment were as rich and tangled as the dense tropical foliage surrounding the little shack, but all I said to Carlos was, "Where's the shower?"

Carlos looked a little bemused, too. He had set his bag in the sleeping area on top of the concrete bed.

"Jim said the shower's the best part," he answered. "It's outside. Let's go look."

Three broad wooden steps led down from the living area to the sand, and a few yards away, off to the right, was a bamboo enclosure about four feet high, above which extended a showerhead at the end of a metal pipe. Purple bougainvillea sprayed over the near wall of the enclosure. On the damp sand under the bougainvillea, in a narrow patch of shade, Señora lay patiently. The air was heavy with the tropical midday heat. I could see a few other houses scattered along the beach like shells. Two surfers floated lazily in the gulf, graceful silhouettes against a shimmering sea.

"Let's swim!" I was already up the wooden stairs and digging in my bag for my bathing suit.

"You go ahead," Carlos said. "I'm going to just unwind a little." He sat down on the top stair and turned his Padres cap around so that the brim shaded his eyes. I pulled my suit on, leaving my sundress draped over one of the leather chairs, and sat down beside him.

"It's a great spot," I said, touching his thigh. He took my hand and held it, and we both watched the surf roll in. The heat and the rhythmic sound of waves crept over me like a spell. I lapsed into a kind of trance; time slowed and then stopped.

Suddenly, my reverie was broken by a squawk and a quick, light pressure on my right shoulder. With a start, I shook my arm and looked around for the source of the invasion. A bright bird fluttered up a few inches away, and landed once again on the hollow of my collar bone.

"Carlos!" I cried. "A parrot!"

Carlos reached out a finger toward the bird, who shuffled across my clavicle away from his touch.

"Hey, Pedrito Perico," Carlos crooned. He made little kissing noises at the parrot. Pedrito hunkered down on my shoulder, unimpressed. "Looks like he's yours," Carlos observed.

"I'm not sure I want him." I smiled a little shakily.

"I'm not sure you have a choice," Carlos said.

"Well, I'm going swimming anyway," I announced. I lifted my left index finger to my right shoulder, and the parrot obediently stepped on. "Sorry, Pete," I told him, shoving him unceremoniously onto the sand.

As I jogged down the beach to the water, I heard Carlos laughing. Looking back, I saw a small puff of crimson and green waddling behind me as fast as its short little legs would go. When I emerged from my swim, twenty minutes later, the parrot was standing at the shoreline, waiting faithfully. He fluttered up to my shoulder with a scolding squawk, and sulked all the way back to the house. When I tried out the lovely outdoor shower, he sat on the top of the bamboo wall and watched me. For the rest of our stay in San José, he was to be my constant companion, leaving me only at night to sleep in the palm tree at the north corner of the house. Carlos jokingly suggested that the bird was the spirit of some former lover, come back to haunt me. I wondered if perhaps it was the spirit of San José himself, come to guide me safely through the lotus lands of Los Cabos.

On the open shelves in the kitchen, we found some cans of tuna and some crackers, as well as a couple of jars of palm hearts. The refrigerator contained two Pepsis and one bottle of Pacifico beer. We made a light lunch of whatever we could find while Señora, too dignified to beg, lay curled at our feet under the old wooden table, one eye watching our every move. There were plenty of scraps for her, and some cracker crumbs for Pedrito. After lunch, we did what everyone who lives in the tropics does during the hottest part of the day: We lay down for a long siesta.

"Shake out your dress before you put it back on," Carlos told me when we woke up a few hours later. "The *alacranes* live in these thatch roofs, and sometimes they get into your clothes."

"What's an *alacrán*?" I asked sleepily. By way of an answer, Carlos took my hand and led me into the living area. In a dim corner by the back wall, he pointed to the floor. A small insect moved languidly in the shadows. I crouched down to get a better look.

"Careful," Carlos warned, at the same time as I gasped, "Oh my God, it's a scorpion!"

"He won't hurt you if you don't bother him," Carlos said calmly. "You just have to remember to shake out your clothes and your shoes before you put them on." A rustle behind me made me turn my head in time to see another scorpion fall from the roof onto the floor with a soft *plop*.

"I guess if Señora can live with these monsters, I can, too," I muttered determinedly.

"That's my girl." Carlos smiled, put an arm around my shoulder, and led me away from the pale, deadly creatures.

By 4:00 P.M., the heat of the day had eased. We drove north toward San José to explore and to stock up on provisions. On the way to town, we passed the elegant old Palmilla, the first hotel to have been built on the cape. Carlos turned up the long winding drive.

Like a dowager queen, the Palmilla reposes among lush tropical gardens that slope down to the sea. Inside, the spacious public rooms exude the air of a more leisurely past. At the polished wood bar, the specialty of the day was *pitahaya* daiquiris made from the fruit of the organ-pipe cactus on which the natives used to gorge themselves during the summer months. Sipping my daiquiri and watching the sun dance on the emerald waters of the Gulf, I recalled descriptions I had read of the orgies of *pitahaya* season. The padres had deplored the decadence of the Baja Indians who, in their eyes, spent most of the year in somnolent languor, waking up only to feast on the sweet cactus fruit and mate during the yearly tribal gatherings. In fact, the *pitahaya* festivals sounded to me like Mardi Gras or Christmas holidays: a few weeks of pleasure in an otherwise grinding yearly cycle devoted to the harsh business of survival.

San José del Cabo still retains the charm of a small Mexican town. Its plaza is shaded by broad leafy trees and surrounded by old colonial buildings. The church, built in this century, is a passable reproduction of the original eighteenth century mission church. Painted tiles on the façade depict the martyrdom of Father Tamaral. About a mile east of town, close to the sea, a large freshwater lagoon dozes beneath towering palms. Fed by an underground river, the lagoon at San José was the only reliable source of fresh water on the cape during the early days; the old Spanish maps call it *Aguada Segura*. On that August afternoon of 1985, the only building on the lagoon was the El Presidente Hotel, although within a few years there would be a parade of modern hotels stretching from the edge of the lagoon down to the beach. Ducks drifted peacefully among the rushes, and cormorants stood like living question marks along the shore.

We found the local market and wandered through rainbows of tropical fruits and chiles of every size and color. American rock music competed with ranchero tunes on the vendors' radios and Sony tape decks. Piñatas and lacy communion dresses hung beside a bunch of dead chickens dangling by their feet. From the interior mazes of the market drifted the pungent odors of *pozole* and *masa*, pork soup and corn meal. By the time we had stowed our purchases in the trunk of the car, twilight was streaking the sky with lavender and gold, and I was hungry for dinner.

A young French couple from Paris had just opened a restaurant near the plaza. There, as the tropical night descended over that distant New World outpost, we dined on *pâté de fois gras* and medallions of beef in delicate pastry puffs and warm baguettes with sweet butter.

The burgundy wine was so smooth that we finished a whole bottle before dessert: Mexican flan adorned with strips of papaya and bathed in Grand Marnier.

It was late when we got home. The night was soft, full of whispers. Little pools of moonlight dappled the living-room floor. Before us, the sand glowed like mother-of-pearl, and a path of spun silver shimmered over the sea. In the little bedroom, the soft curtain billowed like a sail, bearing us through the warm and singing darkness down to a radiant shore.

Over the next three days, we explored the cape area in our rented VW bug. We swam in the crystalline waters and snorkeled among gardens of neon-colored fishes, brilliant gorgonians, and delicate, pastel sea fans. We bought fresh fish from the *pangas* that came up onto the beach near Todos Santos, and we had them cooked in a little roadside restaurant that was no more than a family's kitchen with an extra table or two. We absorbed the slow, timeless pageant of life in the plaza of Todos Santos and wandered among the nearby mango orchards and sugarcane fields beneath the Tropic of Cancer. And in Cabo San Lucas, we watched the sun set over two oceans from the veranda of the Hotel Finisterra, which means Land's End, and where the piña coladas were better than ever again.

When John Steinbeck and Ed Ricketts visited Cabo San Lucas in 1940, it was a settlement of about three hundred fifty souls, most of whom fished or worked at the local cannery. In his book *The Log from the Sea of Cortez*, Steinbeck wrote the following account of that visit:

"It was a sad little town, for a winter storm and a great surf had wrecked it in a single night . . . The road to the little town, two wheelruts in the dust, tossed us about . . . The cactus and thorny shrubs ripped at the car as we went by. At last we stopped in front of a mournful cantina where morose young men hung about waiting for something to happen. They had waited a long time—several generations—for something to happen, these good-looking young men. In their eyes there was a hopelessness . . . Then we happened to them."

Today, there are still such sad little towns scattered through the vast wilderness of Baja, but Cabo San Lucas is no longer one of them. The children and grandchildren of those sad-eyed young men now work in the luxury hotels or the American restaurants and shops that have exploded in the once dreary fishing settlement at the peninsula's tip. And who is to say that they are not better off than were their morose forebears? In the late 1950s, when the first hotels began to appear, there was no airport, nor even a decent road. The founding fathers of what is now a major international tourist destination fought for their dream of development, and the local ranchers supported that dream in every way they could.

But Luis Bulnes, one of the original landowners and developers of the region, told a magazine reporter in 1992, "We spent many years fighting to bring civilization here. Now sometimes I wake up in the middle of the night and wonder if we did the right thing or not. Because, before, you could sleep anywhere and nobody bothered you. If you had a problem, anyone would help you. If you had a flat tire, the first person who passed by would stop to help. Today this has changed."

By Saturday afternoon we had grown tired of driving about and were content to stroll along our own beach and float in our own ocean. Señora and Pedrito had become family, the little shack had become home, and even the occasional soft *plop* of a falling scorpion had become a familiar background sound.

Then the *chubasco* came.

At first, there was just a darkening on the horizon, a subtle shift in the wind. Then whitecaps scuttled across the water. The palm trees began to rustle, then to sway, and finally to bend and groan. The parrot gave a shudder and flew up to disappear among the coconuts. Señora whined and slunk off with her tail between her legs. Like massive gray mountains, storm clouds billowed in from the southeast, filling the sky.

"Looks like it might rain," observed Carlos, and we headed for cover under our *palapa*.

I had never seen so much water. It came down in curtains, in buckets, in torrents, in rivers. It beat on the palm leaves over our heads until even the scorpions seemed to crawl into their secret crevices and disappear. All afternoon it rained, and when we went to bed it was still raining, and the wind was still howling around the corners of the house.

On Sunday morning when we got up, it was still raining.

"Don't bother packing," Carlos told me. "We're not going anywhere today."

"But our flight leaves at 11:00," I protested. "We've got to get to the airport."

"*Mi amor*," said Carlos patiently, "go look at the *pinche* driveway. It's a *pinche* swamp. Even if the airport were open, which I'm sure it's not, we'd never get the *pinche* car to the highway."

"But I have to be at work tomorrow," I squealed. "I have patients scheduled!"

Carlos gazed at me with a look of incredulity mixed with pity. He shook his head.

"Forget it," he said. "Come on. Let's make some coffee."

The storm continued all day. We sat on the leather chairs by the *palapa*'s edge and watched the clouds roll in and the rain come down and the palm trees dance for us alone. It was as if the whole world had shrunk down to the little patch of beach in front of us. It was as if we were the only man and only woman on earth.

In the late afternoon we started drinking beer. Señora lay curled at our feet. A fine spray of warm rain blew in and a wet clean smell drifted up from the beach. In the distance, thunder rumbled. The light was heavy and strange.

Then Carlos said, "Would you marry me?"

Through the long silence that followed, the wind shook the high leaves of the palm trees in fierce gusts and the surf thundered its awesome power. Carlos asked again, softly, this time in Spanish. Señora rose and stretched, circled once, and settled at our feet again with a sigh.

Finally, I found my voice. "This is like a dream, Carlos," I whispered. "This isn't real. Ask me again when we get home."

He did ask me again, on a Wednesday morning in November while he was shaving and I was brushing my teeth. I sat on the bathroom floor and cried a little, and then I said Yes. We were married the following April in my living room, with our kids gathered around us. Carlos's mother came up from Mexico for the occasion. The Shaffers and the Carters were there, and, of course, Marge and Eddie.

A judge took care of the legal details, but Jorge married us in a bilingual ceremony, invoking the blessings of an ecumenical god. Afterward we ate turkey in *mole* sauce and drank champagne. Jorge played his guitar, and we all sang "*De Colores*," the song about springtime fields and rainbows and about great and many-colored loves.

Ensenada

*Ave querida, amada peregrina
mi corazón al tuyo estrecharé.
Oiré tu canto, tierna golondrina
recordaré mi patria y lloraré.*

Dear bird, beloved pilgrim,
my heart reaches out to yours.
I'll hear your song, tender swallow,
I'll recall my country, and I'll weep.

—Narciso Serradel, "Las Golondrinas"

M y new mother-in-law was a tiny woman, delicate and faded as a little house finch. Maybe that's why I didn't notice at first that she was moving in.

After the wedding, when Charley went back to college, Rosa nested in Charley's old room with a proprietary air. But I chose to ignore the signs and assumed that she was planning to stay for a week or two, as my family did when they came to California. I treated Rosa with the careful courtesy one reserves for temporary house guests. Early one morning, however, when I found her sweeping the sidewalk in front of the house, I chided her for working when she was on vacation. She looked at me with the same liquid bronze eyes with which Carlos had always been able to silence me.

"I am not here on vacation," she told me gently. "*Estoy en mi propia casa.*"

That should have been a big clue. "I'm in my own house" was as clear a statement as she could have made. But it wasn't until five months later, after the kids had gone back to school in September, that I finally asked Carlos how long his mother was planning to stay. He rattled the newspaper irritably and didn't look up. That was my answer: He had no idea how long she was going to stay and had no intention of discussing the matter. My gringo obsession with calendars and clocks and numbers was of no interest to him.

In the course of my work with Mexican families at the clinic, I had become acutely aware of how often I requested numerical information and how strange those requests seemed to many of my patients. Especially for *campesino* families from remote rural areas, my questions bordered on the incomprehensible. When I would inquire, for example, how many children a woman had, she might answer vaguely with a litany of names: *Pues, a ver, Juan y luego María y luego Lupe y José . . .* It would be up to me to keep count of the recitation and enter the appropriate number in the appropriate box on my checklist. Then there were the men and women who, when asked their age, would respond by telling me the year they were born ("*Soy de cincuenta y ocho,*") leaving it to me to perform the calculations. Eventually, I began to regard my own questions with the same tolerant amusement with which my patients seemed to regard them. Why were all these numbers so important, anyway? How much meaningful human information could really be obtained by asking the question "How many?"

So I tried to adjust to the idea that my mother-in-law would be with us for an indeterminate length of time, and I tried to adopt a more Mexican attitude—living in the present without dwelling on clocks and calendars. In fact, when I stopped counting, Rosa's presence in the household began to seem as natural as the fragrance of corn tortillas that had begun to permeate the air.

She taught me how to make *menudo,* a popular soup made from the unlikely combination of hominy and cow's stomach, usually served for Sunday brunch. She tried to teach me to make tortillas, but we both gave up after I burned my third batch. I tried to teach her to use the washing machine and dryer, but she never really trusted them and insisted on washing Carlos's underwear by hand. When I found her ironing his jockey shorts, however, I had to draw the line.

"Rosa! What are you doing?"

"Ironing, *hija.*"

"We don't iron underwear here." I sounded arrogant, even to myself. Rosa bent her head and continued ironing.

"*Descansa, hija,*" she told me, "Go and rest. You've had a hard day at work."

Goddamn it, I thought, *she's not going to send me out of my own kitchen.* I went to the stove and turned on the tea kettle, then shuffled impatiently through the pile of mail I had brought in. "Take a break, Rosa," I said, trying for a conciliatory tone. "Let's have a cup of tea."

Rosa set the iron up on its end and smoothed the last pair of jockey shorts onto the freshly laundered stack. Then she went out the back door, returning a moment later with a handful of leaves from the lemon tree. She dropped them into the teapot. "*Hoja de limón,*" she explained, "*es buena para los nervios.*"

I didn't know whether or not lemon leaf tea was really good for nerves, but I was willing to try. We sat at the kitchen table gazing at each other over steaming cups.

"I was like you," Rosa began. "I was always so busy when Carlos and his brother were young. I never had time to take care of them in the way I wanted to."

Rosa had been a teacher during the years immediately following the Mexican Revolution, and she had worked with passionate devotion to bring the light of learning to Mexico's poor. Under the new government, idealistic young *maestras* like Rosa had been sent out to remote villages and ranches where they would hold classes beneath trees, or in barns, or wherever the students would come. Local peasants housed her and fed her and sometimes hid her when the enemies of the revolution rode through the countryside in search of subversive teachers.

"The mothers would bring their children from the fields," Rosa told me. Her eyes glowed with the warmth of a distant sun. "'*Maestra,*' they would say, 'here is my child. Educate him.'"

Only Carlos and his brother had been as important to her as her profession, and Rosa had found no time or space in her life for a husband. In a world of traditional gender roles, she had managed, with quiet dignity, to succeed both as a single mother and as an educator. But always, she told me, she had dreamed of the day when she could retire and make a real home for her sons. Just as that day came, Carlos moved to California and his brother married. . . . "*Pues, en fin,*" she concluded, "it is a small pleasure for me now to iron my boy's underwear. Someday you will feel the same way about Josh."

Rosa's slender brown fingers trembled a little as she raised her cup to her lips. She kept her eyes lowered, and I blinked my own eyes against salty tears. I felt ashamed.

"*Mamá,*" I said, when I could speak, "Would you iron my white silk blouse for me? I always make such a mess of it."

Unobtrusively, Rosa filled our house with her own *sabor*. The kitchen radio was always tuned to one of the Mexican stations that played old romantic trios. Cathy and Josh began looking forward to the daily *telenovelas,* the Mexican soap operas that Rosa watched faithfully. While she watched, she knitted, and soon everyone in the family was wearing custom-made wool slippers. After the slippers, she created afghans for every bed in the house. Then she began to crochet borders on all our cloth napkins, making "tortilla towels" for her homemade tortillas. Sometimes, in the evenings, she would lie on the living-room floor in her long flannel nightgown and do sit-ups.

"Man," said Josh, "she's awesome!"

Cathy said, "I hope I can do sit-ups when I'm eighty."

"Seventy-nine, *hija*," Rosa said from the floor. "Only seventy-nine."

Rosa loved outings. Sometimes I would take her to Kmart to buy yarn for her afghans and creams for her skin, which she kept incredibly smooth and soft. Sometimes she and I would make a foray into Tijuana where she would guide me through the labyrinthine old market, filling her nylon shopping bag with a dazzling array of chiles, fresh cheeses, and strange dried herbs from the old women whose stalls were always in the dimmest corners. Sometimes Carlos and I would take her to a Padres baseball game, and she would sing "The Star Spangled Banner" proudly, with a fine vibrato, although the words she sang were all her own invention. But of all our outings, her favorites were the trips to Ensenada where her sister and brother-in-law from Los Angeles had a second home, and where she felt completely comfortable, back in her own beloved *tierra mexicana.*

From the north, the road into Ensenada sweeps down from breathtaking heights above rocky sea cliffs, then hugs the shoreline and eventually opens into a broad waterfront boulevard graced on the right by bright fishing boats and stately cruise ships, on the left by resort hotels and restaurants. A few blocks away, the one other tourist street in town bustles with young gringos crowding the honky-tonks and visitors plying the curio shops for painted clay bowls and hand-embroidered blouses.

But the rest of Ensenada is a quiet little provincial town, described by the Mexican writer Fernando Jordán as the eye of the peninsula. With patient equanimity, that eye gazes east to the deep shadows of mysterious mountains, west to the shifting sea, south to the fierce and ancient desert, and north to that other desert, equally fierce, of Tijuana and the borderlands beyond.

The eye of Baja California, Jordán said, and the crossroads. For generations Ensenada has been both a point of departure and a beacon of return, a dependable center of civilization in a rugged frontier.

For the prospectors who flocked to the Sierra Juárez to mine her slopes in search of gold, Ensenada was the haven to which they came— hungry, dirty, and usually empty-handed—for a hot bath, a cold beer, and a new pickax. For the farmers who mine the rich river bottom of the Mexicali valley, Ensenada has been the international seaport from which to ship their crops to the world. For the fishermen who follow the schools of yellowtail over the waters beyond the last island on the horizon, the lights in Ensenada's wide, hospitable harbor still glow with the promise of home.

For Carlos's *tío*, Felipe, Ensenada had always been a dream.

"The *pinches paracaidistas* almost did him in," Carlos told me as we sped south on the modern highway between Tijuana and Ensenada.

"The goddamn parachutists? What are you talking about?"

"A *paracaidista* is someone who just shows up and takes over the land," Carlos said, "like a parachutist dropping out of the sky."

"Isn't that legal here?" From the history I had read, I had the impression that it was. After the Mexican-American War, in which Mexico lost more than half of her territory to the U.S., the northern regions of the Baja Peninsula seemed particularly vulnerable to further invasion. To protect against this, the Mexican government offered land, virtually free, to anyone who would colonize it. All that was required, in exchange for land rights, was the guarantee of a minimum number of settlers within a specified number of years. The policy attracted a variety of adventurers and opportunists from the Mexican mainland, as well as capitalists, malcontents, and dreamers from around the world.

Tío Felipe was both a Mexican and a dreamer. Born in Mexicali, he had, as a young man, simply walked into the U.S. along the one-lane rural road that led across the border in those days. He had started out picking oranges in the San Fernando Valley. When the war came, he entered the army as naturally as he had entered the country, fighting with the Allies in the uniform of an American soldier. Afterward, he had worked in construction and had finally become a highly skilled union worker, laying the giant underground pipes that brought water to the new cities of Los Angeles County. He and Tía Yolanda, Rosa's youngest sister, had settled in East L.A., where they raised three children and where, by the time I knew Carlos, they were bouncing grandchildren on their knees.

But Felipe had always cherished the dream that one day he would return to his roots and would make a home for his family in Mexico. To that end, he had acquired two hundred acres of ranch land in the fertile valley of Ojos Negros southeast of Ensenada. For years Felipe had toiled through the workweek in Los Angeles, heading south each Friday night for the six-hour drive to his Mexican homestead. There he would spend the weekend clearing brush, digging post holes, drilling wells, plowing and planting and pruning.

Carlos remembered the coffee.

"*Mi tío* was always up at 5:30 in the morning," Carlos told me, "and he always made a big pot of the best coffee I ever had. Maybe it was the water: It was so pure."

"Where was Yolanda?" I asked.

"She and the kids never wanted to come down there." Carlos shook his head. "My poor *tío*. He worked so hard and dreamed so big, and he could never accept that his family had really become American. They didn't want to drive all that way to some little ranch in Baja. Hell, there wasn't even any TV!"

"What did you used to do when you went down?" I knew that, as a college student in L.A., Carlos had often accompanied his uncle during the weekends.

"It was so beautiful there." Carlos's eyes glowed with the same light I had seen in Rosa's when she spoke of her life as a young teacher. "I loved to help *mi tío* in the fields. I loved to drink coffee with him." Carlos grinned and glanced at me from the corner of his eye. "And I loved to ride El Diablo."

"OK, I'll bite. Who's El Diablo?"

"A big black horse, as wild as a *chubasco*. I was the only one who could ride him."

"Oh sure," I chortled. "Carlos the cowboy. Are you sure El Diablo wasn't a VW van?"

"What do you know about it?" asked Carlos, and he scowled at the road.

"What became of the ranch?" I decided to change the subject. That was when Carlos told me about the *paracaidistas.*

"Felipe couldn't be there all the time," he explained, "and eventually the squatters moved in. They took over, little by little. Finally *mi tío* sold out to them and just walked away.

"*¡Qué lástima!* What a shame," I said.

"But then he bought the *casita* in Ensenada," Carlos added. "So he still feels like a real *bajacaliforniano*. And he knows the best fish taco stand in town!"

It was true. Whenever we went to Ensenada to visit Felipe and Yolanda, we would have at least one meal at the little white cart on the corner of Calle Juárez and Espinoza. The five wooden bar stools at the counter were always full, and the surrounding sidewalk was always jammed with locals clamoring for fish tacos. We learned that we had to arrive before 2:00 in the afternoon; after that, the day's supply would be sold out. In the late 1980s, fish tacos were becoming a fashionable menu item in the upscale restaurants of La Jolla and Laguna Beach. But Juanita, the plump, white-aproned owner of the no-name taco stand in Ensenada, had created the original recipe. Having sampled the real thing, I could never take the imitators seriously.

The fish taco stand was only one of Felipe's Ensenada secrets. Another was the wine country. On a magnificent Saturday in May, when their daughter Jo was visiting with her two little boys, Felipe and Yolanda took us all to the Guadalupe Valley, a peaceful stretch of countryside between Ensenada and Tecate where, in the first decade of the century, a group of Russian settlers had taken advantage of Mexico's open land policy and had started what became known as "The Russian Colony." Graceful silver-green olive trees lined the road, and beyond them, as far as the eye could see, vineyards lay like a verdant carpet adorned here and there with roses in soft pastel shades.

Felipe pulled into a rutted driveway; its rural mailbox announced *Casa Minkoff.*

"Minkoff?" I queried. "That's not a very Mexican sounding name."

"El Señor Pedro Minkoff is as Mexican as a *chile verde*," Felipe assured me. "He was born and raised here in the valley. His kids go to school in Ensenada."

Blond and blue-eyed and thoroughly Mexican, Señor Minkoff seemed delighted that ten people, eight of them strangers, had arrived unannounced at his home in the middle of a Saturday afternoon. Despite his muddy boots and dusty cap, he treated Rosa and Yolanda to a dose of continental charm, kissing their hands until they both blushed like schoolgirls. Cathy and Josh, usually far too cool to revert to playground games, took turns swinging with Jo's kids on the tire that hung from a gnarled olive branch. The rest of us followed Pedro on a meandering tour of his vineyard. We all ended up in the farmhouse kitchen where Pedro poured us samples of the wines that he had opened the evening before for his family's meal. We left with a case of his best vintage.

Back in Ensenada, Carlos and Felipe distributed bottles of wine to the neighbors while Rosa and Yolanda started dinner. That night we all slept together, the generations intertwined. Rosa and Yolanda held hands, whispering and giggling together far into the night. Later, when those times were lost forever, I would remember Rosa as she had been that day, soft and tender as a little girl.

The day Rosa broke her hip did not start out like any other day. It started out worse than most.

For one thing, it was a Monday. The previous Friday, we had driven Rosa to Ensenada where she planned to stay for a couple of weeks during her sister's annual vacation. I had been looking forward to having my kitchen and my husband to myself for those two weeks. But as we headed home Sunday night, we entered a nightmare of long lines and angry drivers waiting to cross the border. Carlos was soon honking and swearing with the rest.

"Jeez, Carlos, you're turning into a gringo," I told him.

"Did you see that asshole?" he yelled.

I didn't answer. The rest of the evening had passed in tense silence, and that night I slept badly.

Then, as I was donning my white lab coat in my office on Monday morning, my secretary stuck her head in the door.

"Steve Carlton's office on line one for you," she said. "I thought you'd want to take the call. They have Annie Harper in there now."

I picked up the phone.

"This is Tammy in Dr. Carlton's office," said a girlish voice. "Dr. Carlton wants me to ask you who's going to pay for the surgery on Annie."

Who indeed? Annie Harper was four years old. She had suffered from recurring ear infections for as long as I had known her, most of her life. A recent hearing test had shown hearing loss in both ears caused by her chronic infections. A simple operation, the insertion of tiny tubes in both eardrums, would almost certainly relieve her condition and restore her hearing. The only problem was that Annie's father had recently started his own business, a small print shop. He had taken out a second mortgage on his home to buy his startup equipment, and he couldn't even consider the three hundred dollars a month it would have cost him to buy health insurance for his family. They still owed me for their past six visits, and I had charged them the lowest rates the hospital would allow.

"Let me speak to Dr. Carlton, please, Tammy." Steve Carlton had been a pediatric resident when I had first come on staff at Children's Hospital, so I had been one of his mentors before he became an ear, nose, and throat specialist. There were some advantages to getting older, I mused.

By the time I had convinced Steve Carlton to let the family pay him in installments, my beeper was blasting frantically. It was the intensive-care nursery. A two-pound premature baby had just gone into cardiac arrest. The little newborn, not much bigger than the palm of my hand, lay in his incubator like a sad rag doll, connected by yards of hard plastic tubing to the world outside. I did what I had to do, mechanically, with a heavy heart. Even if we pulled him through the next few days, I knew the long-term outlook for the child was bleak. No one born so tiny was ever meant to survive, I thought, as I readjusted the breathing tube around his delicate nose. What kind of system spends millions of dollars on two-pound preemies and denies healthy children a chance at normal hearing? I was muttering to myself as I peeled off my gloves and mask and headed down the antiseptic corridor.

I had just returned to my office and was looking over the list of regularly scheduled patients when my secretary appeared again.

"Sorry," she said, "but there's a long-distance call for you on line two. Someone sounds pretty upset."

"Yes?" I barked into the phone. I heard the buzz of static over a long-distance line.

"It's Jo," said a small, scared voice. "I'm here at the ISSTE hospital in Ensenada with my mom . . . " Her voice broke, and she started to sob.

"Jo!" I cried. "What's happened?"

"It's Rosa," she whimpered. "She was hanging some wash on the line to dry, and she slipped, and . . . and . . . "

"Jo." I put on my firm doctor's voice. "Calm down. Just tell me what's going on."

"My dad brought her here to the hospital. They say she broke her hip. They want to operate, but we didn't want to do anything without Carlos. Oh, please, can you come down right away?"

My mind raced, reflex medical reactions whirling among vivid, random images. Elderly female, fractured hip: Operate within first twelve hours to restore mobility as soon as possible; avoid complications of pneumonia and deep venous thrombosis. Rosa, her white hair like a shaggy halo, bargaining lustily with the produce man in the market over the price of a *chile ancho*. Crispy *buñuelos* covering every inch of my kitchen counter space at Christmastime, filling the house with the pungent scent of cinnamon.

"Of course, Jo," I said softly to the telephone. "Don't worry. We'll be there as soon as we possibly can."

The hospital in Ensenada was a low, ugly stucco structure huddled between a supermarket and a beauty salon. The lobby was dim and smelled of mildew. Rosa's room was at the end of a maze of dingy corridors.

It was really more like a cubicle than a room, windowless and only slightly larger than the narrow bed in which Rosa lay. Her white face and white hair seemed to fade into the sheets, and at first, all I could see were her eyes, wide and dark with terror. When I bent over and hugged her, she felt as insubstantial as a sparrow.

"*Mamá,*" I whispered. "Are you in pain?"

"No, *mi'ja.*" Rosa managed a faint smile. Without her dentures, she looked withered and ancient. "They have my leg in traction, so it doesn't hurt."

I glanced down. Rosa's right leg was elevated to about thirty degrees by a sheet looped around her knee and around the metal bar at the foot of the bed. On the other end of the sheet hung a plastic one-gallon water bottle, half full. I looked wordlessly at Carlos. He shrugged.

"Ensenada," he said, as if I needed to be reminded of where we were.

We stayed with Rosa through the long afternoon, perched on her bed where we could hold her hand. A few minutes after we arrived, Yolanda and Jo and the boys burst in with bags of food from a nearby restaurant. The thin hospital blanket was soon stained with salsa, and the tiny cubicle smelled of fresh tortillas and chiles. Rosa almost disappeared among the mounds of half-eaten tacos and the solicitous family members crowded onto her bed. When the radiology technician showed up with a portable X-ray machine, it took a full five minutes to make room for her in the cubicle.

In urgent, whispered conferences we had all been trying to decide whether to transport Rosa across the border so that she could benefit from U.S. medical technology. I was in favor of the idea.

"But you wouldn't be able to visit your *abuelita* on the other side," I warned Jo's boys. "They don't let children into patients' rooms."

"No way!" said David, the ten-year-old.

"Why not?" Jimmy was eight, young enough to ask the obvious.

"Could we bring her tacos?" asked Yolanda, close to tears. "You know she can't get well on gringo food."

"Mom," said Jo, "don't be silly. That's not the issue."

Carlos didn't say anything, but I could see that he was thinking. And he never took his eyes off Rosa's face. After the X-ray technician left, he finally spoke.

"I think she's better off here," he said. We all looked at him. "Did you see how scared she was of that little portable X-ray machine? An MRI scan would probably kill her! I say we leave her here, where at least she feels at home."

"OK," I said reluctantly, "but in that case, I want to meet the orthopedic surgeon."

Dr. Alvarez looked frighteningly young to me, but he exuded confidence. Although it was almost 5:00 in the afternoon, his white lab coat was as fresh as if Rosa herself had laundered and pressed it, and his thick black hair gleamed.

"Oh yes, *señora*," he assured me, "I have performed that surgery several times. It is actually quite simple." He rubbed his hands together gleefully, as if in anticipation.

"Well, then," I said, wondering just how many "several times" meant. "I guess you'll be operating tomorrow morning?"

"Oh no, *señora*," answered the doctor, his dazzling smile undimmed. "I do not have the proper instruments here. I must order them from Mexico City."

"Mexico City! How long will that take?"

"Ten days," he said, matter-of-factly. "Perhaps two weeks."

"What?" I yelped. Carlos took my elbow, but I was too far gone to heed his silent warning. "What kind of medicine do you people practice here?" I had unconsciously lapsed from Spanish into English. Later, I reflected that I had probably sounded to Dr. Alvarez like a gringo version of Ricky Ricardo unleashing at Lucy a torrent of Cuban expletives. But the young doctor's courtly manners never wavered. He simply stood there, listening quietly while I ranted on about the proper treatment of hip fractures.

"*Claro*," he said, when I paused for breath. "Of course, *señora*, you are completely correct. That is how I was trained in Guadalajara. But here in the provinces we must practice differently. There is much need, and there are few resources . . . " Not enough resources to meet the needs. That was a concept with which I was all too familiar. My heart rate began to return to normal.

" . . . Of course," the doctor was saying, "if, by chance, you could obtain the surgical instruments *en el otro lado* . . . "

I looked at Carlos. Carlos looked at me.

"I don't know," I said, "I've never had to go scrounging for my own equipment. I wouldn't know where to begin."

"We'll find whatever you need, Doctor," said Carlos, extending his hand. "*Gracias.*"

From my office the next day, I placed calls to every orthopedic surgeon I knew and several that I didn't know. It was after 4:00 P.M. when I finally tracked down a surgical supply wholesaler thirty miles north of San Diego.

"Six hundred dollars," said a hearty male voice on the other end of the line. "That's for the whole hip set. But you probably won't use all the instruments on the tray. We'll buy back whatever you don't use."

"Buy them back?" I asked, astounded. "Can you do that?"

The man just laughed. "I'm closing now," he said. "If you want the set, come in tomorrow morning after 10:00."

By noon on Wednesday, we were speeding south again with a flat, rectangular package wrapped in brown paper and sealed with the black-striped tape that indicated autoclave sterilization. The hip set came with a manual, which Carlos read while I drove.

"This is like carpentry," he remarked. "Hell, I could do this operation. Drills, nails . . . They even have diagrams to show the insertion angles!"

I had always known that Orthopedics was a highly mechanical specialty, but I had never actually thought of it as carpentry.

"Let's hope Alvarez is as optimistic as you are," I said.

Dr. Alvarez was beyond optimistic. When the nurse finally found him, it was 8:00 P.M., and he had started to wilt. But when Carlos handed him the surgical tray, his whole body seemed to light up. He caressed the brown paper with an almost erotic touch, as if his hands were moving on satin. I could sense the longing in his fingers for the smooth, cool hardness of precision instruments. He disappeared down the dim corridor, clutching the precious package to his chest and muttering, "*Mañana . . . mañana . . .*"

But there was to be no surgery the next day, nor the day after that. First, there was the matter of blood.

"No," said the diminutive head nurse when we returned in the morning, "we cannot schedule the operation today. We have not received any blood from the family."

"Do you mean to tell me that in this whole hospital you don't have a couple of pints of O positive blood?" Carlos was holding my elbow again. The nurse gazed at me, unperturbed.

"We have not received any blood from the family," she repeated quietly.

Later, after I had calmed down, I thought of what the doctor had said about so much need and so few resources. I imagined that the little blood they had on hand was probably reserved for trauma cases, young healthy people in need of emergency transfusions. An old lady with a fractured hip was not a priority.

Of course, there was no shortage of volunteers from the family, and by Thursday evening we had donated enough blood to meet the hospital's standards. But the next morning, when Carlos and I arrived at 8:00 to see Rosa before she went to the operating room, we found her eating *pan dulce* in bed and laughing at David's impersonation of Dr. Alvarez.

Carlos headed me off, seeking out the nurse on duty before I could get to her. He returned to the room shortly and beckoned me into the hallway.

"There's a surgical drain they need that they don't have here," he explained, "but the nurse told me where we can buy one in town."

I shrugged, too weary to react. During the past few days, Carlos and I had put hundreds of miles on the car, driving the seventy miles between Ensenada and San Diego half a dozen times. In between trips, we had tried to keep things from falling apart at work and at home. But although we were frazzled, Rosa herself lay like a kind of quiet hurricane's eye, surrounded by raging winds but utterly unruffled by them. Engulfed by vigilant relatives and by endless mounds of food, she radiated a patient serenity that had nothing to do with surgical schedules or medical data. Only when she had to be moved, to use a bedpan or to change a gown, did she cry out in pain. But then an attendant would fill the water bottle a little more, or empty it by a few ounces, adjusting the traction until she was comfortable again.

The store where we went to find the surgical drain was closed for the afternoon meal when we got there. But the owner, who lived next door, opened his shop especially for us when we explained the situation. Later that evening we visited the home of the hospital's medical director to request that he make an exception and open his operating room on a Saturday for Rosa.

As he escorted us out, having promised to make the operating room available only on the condition that none of his nurses had prior family commitments, my head was spinning with bewilderment.

"I feel like Alice in Wonderland," I told Carlos. "I just can't figure out what this crazy Mexican medical system is all about."

Carlos took my hand and stroked it thoughtfully. His eyes were far away and I knew he hadn't really heard me. "I guess," I mused, continuing the conversation with myself, "it's all about people."

Even at the last minute, when Rosa was lying on the gurney the next morning, prepped and ready for surgery, Carlos had to run next door to the beauty salon for nail polish remover to take off the polish that Yolanda had lovingly applied. I bent over the gurney in the dim corridor, scrubbing the pink from her fingernails while Carlos held her other hand and Yolanda caressed her temples. Then the nurse wheeled her away, murmuring endearments like a mother to a small child.

We brought Rosa home a few days later with a shiny new pin in her hip and a deep shadow across her face. She seemed to have collapsed into herself, lying apathetically in bed or propped passively in a chair when we insisted she get up. She was reluctant to use the walker we had brought for her, and she resisted the exercises the physical therapist had taught us. She didn't bother to put her dentures back in her mouth. She barely picked at her food.

Finally Carlos asked, "*Mamá*, are you homesick?" The tears that filled her eyes were answer enough. It was decided that Carlos would fly with her back to Mexico City where his brother Raúl would meet them. Rosa would be reinstalled in her own little house next door to Raúl and his family, in the old neighborhood where everyone still called her *maestra* and where at least one grandchild shared her bed every night.

But somehow, when I stood at the window in the airport watching Rosa turn painfully in her wheelchair to wave a withered hand in farewell, I knew that I would not see her again.

In retrospect, we all agreed that the stomach cancer had probably started when she broke her hip, the same visceral constriction that eats away at wild birds in captivity. Less than a year after we put her on the plane, Raúl phoned one Wednesday night to tell us that Rosa had been vomiting blood and that surgery was planned for the following Monday.

"Don't wait," I told Carlos. "Go see your mom now."

She died on Easter Sunday, *el domingo de la resurección,* escaping the surgeon's knife in the end. I flew down to join the family for her funeral.

We buried her in Aguascalientes, under a shady tree with her mother and a brother who had gone before. After a memorial service in the little church built by Carlos's grandfather, everyone walked the few blocks to the cemetery. Small nieces and nephews ran shouting under new spring leaves. Cousins sparkled in bright dresses and high-heeled shoes; no one wore black. Carlos and Raúl took turns carrying the little box that contained Rosa's ashes, and we stopped at the cemetery's entrance to buy a bunch of Easter lilies from a woman with an infant tied to her back. Several of the children bought ice cream at the cart next to the flower lady.

Afterward, the whole clan gathered for a meal of *carne asada* in cousin Consuelo's patio. The afternoon rang with gossip and laughter, the squeals of children and the occasional squalling of a baby. Just as the sun was sinking down behind the red-tiled roof, a lone swallow swooped out of the sky, skimming low above the assembled family, its wings humming with a fine vibrato.

It was years later that the festering health-care crisis in our own country finally erupted into public consciousness. As I listened to the mounting controversy over the proper allocation of limited resources,

I sometimes thought back to the little hospital room in Ensenada, where pain and hope mingled with the fragrance of tortillas, and where Rosa held us all in an unbroken circle of love.

Punta Cono

Me gusta cantarle al viento
porque vuelan mis cantares
y digo lo que siento
por toditos los lugares.

I love to sing to the wind
because my songs take wing
and I say just what I feel
to all the far-off places.

—Chucho Monge, "La Feria de las Flores"

On a sun-drenched August afternoon in 1991, Cathy married the young man whom she had met four summers before and with whom she had shared her college years. My father, my two sisters, and a favorite aunt flew in from Philadelphia for the wedding, along with a few relatives of Cathy's father. Felipe, Yolanda, and Jo came down from Los Angeles. Carlos's brother, two nieces, one nephew, two cousins, three aunts, an uncle, and their assortment of spouses and children all flew in from Mexico. Dan, the groom, had grown up in our California town, and his family was almost all local.

"Can you handle this?" Marge asked me over margaritas at lunch one day. She was helping me shop for my mother-of-the-bride dress. "You're going to have the Jewish *meschpuchah,* the Mexican *familia,* and Dan's all-American team. Not to mention your ex-husband, his new wife, her relatives, your second husband, his son, your kids . . . " She drained her glass and waved it at the waiter without turning around.

"Don't worry," I answered. "You're the one who used to lecture me on the New Age, remember? One World Family and all that? This is going to be a real '90s wedding."

"Yeah, yeah, I know," said Marge, inserting a Benson & Hedges into a long black cigarette holder. "But you're a '60s chick, like me. Afterward you're going to have a houseful of Jews and Mexicans. How are you going to entertain them all? What are you going to feed them?"

"Well," I told her, "for the morning-after breakfast, I'm serving *menudo* and bagels."

"*Oy vey* and *¡Santa María!*" Marge struck her forehead in mock disgust. "And for lunch, no doubt, you're serving chopped liver tacos!"

It was a wonderful party. My father danced every salsa number with one or another of Carlos's aunts, and the whole Mexican family joined the circle when the Jewish contingent danced the hora. Cathy and Dan and their friends entertained the older generation with a currently popular dance called "the chicken," which involved a great deal of arm-flapping and hip-wiggling. Late in the evening, after the rice had been tossed and the bridal couple had departed for Hawaii, my former husband came over to where I sprawled, exhausted, over a wine-stained, crumb-littered tablecloth. When he laid a gentle hand on my shoulder, his touch was that of a dear old friend.

"She looked so beautiful and so happy," he said. "We did good." Looking up, I saw that his eyes were full of tears.

It was a bittersweet time. Charley had moved into his own apartment near the downtown San Diego office where he worked. Josh had just graduated from high school and was dismantling his room before leaving for college in northern California. Cathy and her new husband had bought a condominium in Orange County, where they had both gone to school and where they now had jobs. As the house settled into a strange silence and a late summer wind blew in from the desert, Carlos and I could feel our lives sliding inexorably toward autumn.

"What's your favorite retirement fantasy?" I asked Carlos one evening over a leisurely supper at our kitchen table. He laughed.

"You used to ask me about other kinds of fantasies!"

"Never mind that, *viejo*," I said fondly. "Be serious. One of these days, we'll have more time on our hands. What would you like to do with it?"

"Well," he mused, "there's still a lot of Baja left to explore. I'd like to travel down there, enjoy it before it all disappears."

"We'd better not wait for retirement," I remarked. "It might not last that long!"

A new season was upon Baja, too, and its changes were as bittersweet as our own. Electricity had long since come to El Rosario, and the road that had washed out in every storm for so many years was now spanned by a modern concrete bridge. At the turnoff for Ejido Eréndira, a billboard advertising oceanfront lots for sale announced, in scarlet letters, MALIBU BEACH SOUTH. The road was paved all the way to the coast, and trucks rolled out of the *ejido* twenty-four hours a day, bringing produce to markets on both sides of the border. Between Tijuana and Ensenada, hundreds of American vacation homes had sprouted up along what had come to be known as "The Gold Coast." Entire communities materialized out of nowhere, many of them surrounded by elaborate walls—apparently designed to keep the residents sealed off from the land in which they chose to live. Carlos grumbled that soon the sea itself would be blocked from view by a giant security fence running the whole length of the peninsula.

"How many of these gringo invaders," he asked rhetorically, "do you think are actually illegal aliens in Mexico?"

Nowhere was the new era more apparent than at the border itself. Where once a barbed-wire fence had run along an open field, there now rose a ten-foot reinforced steel wall erected by the U.S. Army Corps of Engineers. On its north side, beneath a constant glare of floodlights, armed INS vehicles prowled through No Man's Land like hungry beasts of prey. Gone were the hopeful clusters of families along the Mexican side; gone were the brash vendors and the bright blare of music. In their place, a few clusters of grim young men huddled in the shadows, waiting for something to break. Murals in the style of Diego Rivera appeared along the south side of the wall. Near the San Ysidro crossing, someone had painted, in bold white letters, a kind of credo:

Ni ilegales, ni criminales;	Neither illegals nor criminals;
¡trabajadores internacionales!	international workers!

Sometimes, during the long droughts that periodically plague southern California, a coyote will venture out from his canyon to electrify, for a moment, the edge of our civilized world. Driven by hunger and thirst, he may carry off a small dog or a cat; if he is unlucky, he may himself be carried off by a speeding car on a dark freeway or by a farmer defending his livestock.

I knew a woman who once discovered a young coyote wounded

and dying by the side of the road. Somehow she managed to bring him home and nurse him back to health. Afterward she kept him around like a pet dog, and the animal seemed content to stay. When I ventured to ask her one day if she didn't think the coyote might be better off in the wild, she scoffed.

"That's romantic rubbish," she told me. "Life in the state of nature is brutish and short. Look at how glossy his coat is. Look at how plump he's become. With me, he lives a life of comfort. In the wild, he'd probably be dead by now."

Knowing how vulnerable I am to romantic rubbish, I didn't argue with her. But although the creature's coat was glossy and his belly full, his eyes looked dull and lifeless. It was as if, for his wild spirit, a life of comfort had been a kind of death.

Like the woman who tamed the coyote, most *bajacalifornianos* would have considered it romantic rubbish for me to mourn the decline of Baja's wild spirit. Better roads and modern communication were opening up the peninsula, and tourist dollars meant higher living standards for those who lived there. But along those stretches of the old *camino real* known as Mexico Highway 1, satellite dishes bloomed like mutant flowers on ancient *cardón* cacti beside thatch roofed huts, and I couldn't help imagining that, along with the eagles who had once perched on those cacti, the old Baja gods had fled to the distant hills, exiles in their own land. I couldn't help mourning the end of an innocent world, one that had renewed my own spirit so often over the years.

Or perhaps I was mourning for myself. On a Saturday in mid-September, about a month after Cathy's wedding, I drove Josh up to the San Francisco Bay area and helped him move into his new dorm. When I looked back over my shoulder after the last good-bye hug, I saw a tall, gangly stranger leaning against the door frame where I had left my little boy. The battered guitar case on the floor behind him was the only familiar image in that strange new world, and I took comfort from the thought that he had carried with him a little of the old music. But the song that followed me down the corridor from Josh's dorm room was new music, sung by the group called R.E.M. "It's the end of the world as we know it," came a young man's voice, in a distinctly upbeat melody. "It's the end of the world as we know it, and I feel fine!"

Interstate 5 cuts through California like a surgical wound, sterile and hard and efficient. It matched my mood as I drove south from San Francisco, my heart as dull as the empty landscape and the endless highway miles. When I finally pulled up in front of our house late Sunday evening, the windows all looked dark and deserted, and I dreaded the empty rooms inside.

As I approached our bedroom at the back of the house, I saw that one light was burning after all. Carlos was sitting up in bed and peering at a map of Baja over his newly acquired reading glasses. I kicked off my shoes and slid in beside him. Although the night was warm, I felt cold all over.

"We need a Baja trip," he said, after I had given him a tearful account of the weekend. "I was looking at all the territory that's still undeveloped." He bent over the map, pointing. "There's really only one main paved road down most of the peninsula. But there are still plenty of little dirt roads, *gracias a Dios*." He ran a finger down a stretch of Pacific coastline southwest of Cataviña. It looked to be at least fifty miles off the highway. "I'll bet there's still great fishing from these beaches."

Carlos's glasses had slipped down to the end of his nose during his eager scrutiny of the map, and his eyes shone with a combination of excitement and presbyopia.

"*¡Vámonos!*" I said.

We set off a couple of months later in our new Isuzu Trooper, the vehicle which would never really substitute for the old beloved VW vans, but which was much kinder to our aging backs and hips. The Shaffers followed in their new Ford Explorer. We had poured over the map and had carefully highlighted the broken line which denoted an old wagon trail from El Mármol, a once-prosperous onyx mine, to the Pacific coast port where the ore had been loaded onto ships. About twenty miles south, a second broken line led west across the desert to what appeared to be a series of coves enticingly distant from any paved road. Our plan was to stop in Cataviña for gas and for advice from the locals as to road conditions and routes.

From the time of the early Baja missionaries, the region between Tijuana and El Rosario has been known as *la frontera,* an acknowledged transition zone between two worlds. Even with all the changes of modern times, there still exists an invisible boundary line somewhere around the thirtieth parallel. Above that line, Baja California lies in the shadow of *el otro lado* with its relentless march toward progress and its ruthless domestication of all that is wild. But below that line, even now, the magic still lives.

It was early in the morning of our second day out when we passed through El Rosario, now a bustling little town with several motels and restaurants along the highway. Shortly after we crossed the bridge over the once-flooded arroyo, *cirio* trees began to appear, their tips bright with pale yellow, flame-shaped blossoms. The road was better than it had been in years past, but there were still enough potholes to require constant attention.

South of El Rosario, in the vicinity of the thirtieth parallel, we came upon a flock of six enormous buzzards encamped in the middle of the road, enjoying a meal. We rolled to a stop while the huge birds raised slow, disdainful heads to fix us with blood-red eyes. Only after a full minute or two—enough time to establish their dominance of the situation—did they condescend to let us pass, rising with a lugubrious rustle of great wings.

A few miles farther south, we passed the rusted-out skeleton of a car that had failed to negotiate one of the sharp curves; a few miles after that, we came across the unlikely remains of two small boats lying in a narrow wash beside the road.

"Boats?" I asked Carlos. "We're fifty miles from either ocean. Where did they come from?"

"*¿Quién sabe?*" Carlos answered. His face looked relaxed, younger. "We're back in Baja. Nothing should surprise us."

Doña Josefina had died two years before, and although Rancho Santa Inés continued to welcome tourists, we didn't have the heart to go back. Just north of Cataviña, however, we passed a bright purple cottage with a hand-lettered sign reading *RANCHO EL DESCANSO.* Beneath the lettering, someone had drawn the head of a smiling cow and had labeled it *MACHACA.*

"Hmm," Carlos said, "I'm ready for a *descanso*, and *machaca con huevos* sounds pretty good right now. Let's stop."

He made a U-turn and pulled into the yard in front of the sign. The Shaffers' Explorer was already there.

The *machaca* with eggs was as good as I remembered it having been at Rancho Santa Inés, and the coffee was even better. My coffee mug was white with black lettering that said: *NICE BEAUTY SALON, ROWLAND HEIGHTS, CA*. Sue's cup had a scene of The Last Supper painted on it, and Bob and Carlos each had mugs that read *SECURE HORIZONS, JINGLE BELL SENIORS' WALK*.

The little café occupied the front room of the family's home, and the two teenage girls who served us gossiped and giggled in the kitchen while we ate. When we were ready for the bill, the older of the two girls asked us to tell her what we had had, and she wrote it down slowly on a paper napkin, then took it back to the kitchen for help with the addition. Before climbing back into our cars, we went through a gate fashioned from an old bed spring and headed for the outhouses behind the cottage—past chickens scratching in dusty earth and a couple of soft brown burros behind a living fence of nopal cactus.

We were stretching our legs at the Pemex station in Cataviña when the old man materialized, seemingly out of thin air. His long beard was a salt-and-pepper bramble, and his glittering, red-ringed eyes reminded me of the vultures we had seen on the road. He wore a filthy T-shirt, muddy green pants, and ancient boots. His cap, pulled low on his forehead, read *C & S TRUCKING, DUMBARTON, CA*.

"*Buenos días, maestro,*" he greeted Carlos.

"*Buenos días,*" returned Carlos, suspiciously. He put a protective hand on the car's flank, where the attendant was pumping gas.

The old man pulled an object from his pocket and moved close to Carlos. I came up behind in time to see that the object was a black plastic cylinder for storing film. The old man was removing the cap.

Shit, I thought to myself, looking around for cops, *he wants to sell us drugs*.

Inside the cylinder was a single sheet of toilet paper. With infinite tenderness, the old man lifted out the paper and unfolded it in the palm of his hand to reveal a rough metallic nugget, the size and shape of a wad of used chewing gum.

"*Oro,*" breathed the old man, reverently. "Gold. Five grams for two hundred thousand pesos. A special price for you, *maestro.*"

Carlos laughed. "*¿Cómo se llama usted?*" he asked.

The old man broke into a toothless grin. "*Francisco Miguel Martínez, para servirles.*" He extended a grimy hand. "*Todos me dicen El Anima.*"

"The Ghost," I translated to myself. "Why would they call him The Ghost?"

"*¿Por qué El Anima?*" Bob had come over in time to hear the old man's introduction. His own beard was, by now, completely gray and only slightly better groomed than El Anima's.

"Well," the old man explained, "I've been prospecting for gold in these mountains for thirty years." He gestured toward the southeast where the jagged spine of Baja disappeared into a violet haze. "I don't come into town very often, and they've given me up for dead many times. But I always return." He cackled, then coughed and spat. "Like a ghost," he gasped, "*como una ánima.*"

Carlos pulled out our map, indicating the coastline we hoped to explore and the roads we had been considering.

"There's only one road that will get you there," El Anima croaked. "If you take either of these," pointing to the broken lines we had marked, "you'll all be *ánimas del desierto,* desert ghosts!" He grinned like a death's head and started to cough again. "The only road that's passable is the one going north from Santa Rosalillita."

Sue exclaimed, "That's sixty miles out of our way!"

"*Así es, señora,*" agreed El Anima amicably, "that's right. You'll be there in three hours, *con la ayuda de Dios.*"

"We'll take your advice, Don Pancho," said Carlos quickly, extending his hand. "*Muchas gracias. Que te vaya muy bien.*"

As we pulled back onto the road, I observed, "Two hundred thousand pesos for five grams of gold comes to about four hundred dollars an ounce. That's no bargain; that's market price."

"Of course," said Carlos, "What did you expect? These guys probably read *The Wall Street Journal!*"

It was mid-afternoon when we turned onto the gravel road that led from the highway to the fishing village of Santa Rosalillita. After hours of desert travel, the sudden apparition of white crescent beach and turquoise sea looked like a fanciful mirage. But it was real enough. We passed a wooden shack in front of which three bare-chested young men, each with a can of Tecate in his hand, engaged in animated conversation across the open hood of an old pickup truck whose right rear wheel was missing. We passed a tiny white church whose front door, flanked by two giant pink clam shells, opened onto the sea. Then there was nothing but bright water and smooth sand and the soft dunes behind—where tall yuccas rose like Joshua trees, small miracles in a desert garden.

By the time we had made camp, dusk had fallen. We built a fire and toasted Santa Rosalillita with our own Tecates while the little waves lapped gently at the shore. After dinner, we watched the sea come alive with silver light as an almost-full moon rose in the east over El Anima's mountains.

Carlos was awake at dawn and headed down the beach to fish, but the rest of us got up slowly with the sun. By the time the first pot of coffee was ready, Carlos was back, and his mood was foul.

"*Hijos de la chingada*," he swore under his breath, and I knew from the strength of the language, several degrees beyond "son of a bitch," that he was really upset about something.

"You didn't catch anything?" I ventured.

In tense silence, he began dismantling his gear, biting viciously through the fishing line to remove the weights and hooks.

"*¿Qué pasó, hombre?*" asked Bob, mildly.

Carlos exploded. "*Pinches pescadores cabrones*," he yelled, "the goddamn fishermen have the whole frigging bay surrounded by gill nets. There aren't any fish here because those *pinche* gill nets kill everything. Everything. Look!" He swept his arm in a semicircle, indicating the bay that sparkled tranquilly in the morning sun.

I followed his gesture with my eyes. Then I saw them, bobbing on the surface of the water about eighty yards out, a series of little red floats at regular intervals where the gill nets ringed the bay like a deadly corral.

Carlos stowed his fishing pole in the Trooper and began pulling out tent pegs angrily. I brought him a cup of coffee, and he sank into his beach chair, clutching the warm mug in both hands.

"We weren't going to stay here anyway, Carlos," Sue said in her most soothing tone. "We'll just take a swim, have some breakfast, and follow that little dirt road up the coast to Fish Heaven."

"The worst part of it is," Carlos said, calming down, "these *pendejos* are destroying their own future. How are they going to make a living when the fish are gone?"

The rough dirt trail that led to the beaches north of Santa Rosalillita was every bit as bad as we could possibly have wished. Avoiding the rocky headlands along the coast, it meandered through the chaparral about a mile inland, two faint ruts slashed into the rubble of the desert floor. Sometimes it disappeared altogether, and more than once it came to an abrupt stop above precipitous gullies where flash floods had simply sheared the earth away. Carlos was ecstatic.

"This is more like it," he crooned, as he backed away from one of the gullies and turned the vehicle toward what looked like a possible detour. "This reminds me of the good old days."

It reminded me of something I had read in an old Baja history book, a letter from a Jesuit priest to his brother back in Europe. Father Jakob Baegert, in 1752, had described the land he knew as California as "a pathless, waterless, thornful rock, sticking up between two oceans." I kept my thoughts to myself, however, and waited to catch a glimpse of the Pacific Ocean again.

Little by little, with the almost imperceptible tenacity by which spring supplants winter, the rocky trail inched upward and westward toward the coast. As it rose, the landscape softened. Thickets of mesquite trees appeared, luxuriant with butter-yellow blossoms; and elephant trees, once mere clumsy stumps, waved fingers of rosy flowers. A coyote bounded through the chaparral, heading inland along an ancient path. From atop a giant *cardón* cactus, an eagle watched us with unblinking scorn.

Time had vanished, and I had no idea how long we had been driving when we finally crested a ridge and caught sight of the first cove. It lay below us like a dream, miles of white sand along a vast bowl of ocean, shocking in the depth of its blue. But what was more shocking was the isolation of the place. To come upon such a perfect beach, untouched by any sign of human invasion, was almost more than our senses could comprehend.

There were no other vehicles, no tire tracks, no road signs. There were no buildings, nor even any tents. There were no telephone poles or electric wires. There was only the desert, the sky, and the sea, as simple as on the day of their creation. We stopped the car in the middle of the road and got out. Bob and Sue, behind us, had stopped, too, and we all stood together in awe-struck silence. The only sound was the faint murmur of surf and the breath of the desert in our ears.

Finally Sue spoke. "Is this it?" she asked, vaguely. I wasn't sure what she meant by the question.

Bob whispered, "Incredible."

Carlos had his hands thrust deep into the pockets of his faded blue shorts. He seemed to be sniffing the air and gazed to the north. "Let's keep going," he suggested. "I see a point out there . . . ." He indicated with his chin the distant coastline, mauve and gray in the mist. "I can hear the fish calling me!" He grinned, and we all began to chatter at once as we climbed back into the cars.

When we reached Punta Cono, the sun was directly overhead, casting in sharp relief the huge mound of granite that gave the point its name. The road virtually disappeared at the foot of a steep, rocky hill, beyond which stretched a finger of land between pounding surf and a calm, south-facing bay. The car had already been laboring in four-wheel drive; now Carlos threw it into low gear.

"We're not going over this mountain, are we?" I cried. But I already knew the answer, and I closed my eyes as the Trooper inched its way straight up, clinging to the earth like a mountain goat. When I opened my eyes again we had come to a stop in a world of wild beauty, wave-lashed and redolent of the sea, the air thronged with mewing gulls and the soft whir of pelican wings. Sue, pale and trembling, was stumbling out of the Explorer. "I didn't believe it when you started up that hill," she croaked, laying a sweaty palm on my shoulder. "I thought we were all going to die!"

"And give El Anima the last laugh? Not a chance." Bob draped an arm around her. "What a spot!"

"*¿Verdad?*" Carlos said from behind the Trooper. He was already tying knots in his fishing line, his tackle box open on a rock beside him.

That night we dined on fresh fish, grilled over mesquite coals under a canopy of stars. As we were setting the coffeepot over the fire to brew, a voice spoke from the darkness.

"*Buenas noches*," said the voice. None of us had heard footsteps, and we all froze. Out of the shadows and into the flickering light of our camp, two forms emerged. Carlos and Bob were both on their feet instantly.

"*Traemos langosta*," a second voice said. "We bring lobster."

"*¡Langosta!*" Sue cried. "Come and sit down!"

Ignacio and Baltazar perched uncertainly on a mesquite log at the edge of our circle. We offered them beer, and they offered us three small lobsters and six abalone. Slowly, warmed by the fire, the beer, and the light of the rising moon, they began to unfold in halting, self-conscious phrases.

Fishermen from Santa Rosalillita, they shared a *panga* in which they worked a hundred miles of coastline. They were currently staying in a temporary fish camp two miles up the beach, and, besides a handful of other fishermen, we were the only people they had seen for fifteen days.

Baltazar was in his mid-twenties with thick, wavy black hair and a bushy mustache over tobacco-stained teeth. The sleeves of his tattered white T-shirt stretched across biceps covered in tattoos. If I had encountered him on a dark street in San Diego, I mused, I would have crossed to the other side in a hurry. But here on the dark beach, his shy smile flickering in the firelight, he seemed a gentle boy. When I asked him if he had any children, he ducked his head and giggled.

"*Pues*," he answered, "*soy católico*," "I'm Catholic." He fingered the medallion at his neck, Saint Christopher, the protector of travelers and children.

Ignacio, perhaps twice the age of his young partner, had bright, intelligent eyes set deep in a weathered face. He wore an old plaid wool shirt and tight jeans over a sinewy body. A huge barrel chest reflected years of hunting on the ocean floor with only an air compressor and a slender hose linking him to the other side.

Their *panga*, he told us, was twenty years old. A new one would cost two thousand dollars, the motor another three thousand. Each lobster trap cost fifteen dollars to make. They could sell their lobster for three dollars a pound, abalone for seven dollars a pound. But their biggest return came from shark fins which went for fifteen dollars a pound.

"That's why," he explained, as if he had read Carlos's mind, "we use the nets. We know we are killing all the fish. But it is very expensive to send our children to school. They need shoes and books and paper . . . ." His voice trailed off, and he turned his face toward the darkness. When Ignacio spoke again, his words sounded faint and far away, drifting like smoke on the wind. "They have fished these waters for many years," he said. "Have you seen *las conchas de los ancianos*, the shells of the ancient ones?"

We had noticed countless shell middens, broad splashes of white along the rocky shore where generations long past had drawn life from the sea. No one spoke for a time, and the last embers of the fire began to die. "*Ya nos vamos*," Ignacio said finally. "*Que pasen una buena noche.*" Then they were gone, as silently and suddenly as they had appeared.

When we were snugly wrapped in our sleeping bag under our dome tent, I said, "Those guys seemed to come from nowhere and disappear into nowhere."

"Mexicans," said Carlos cryptically, and closed his eyes.

In the morning, we set out to explore. Between our camp and the open sea, tall sand dunes undulated like waves. When we reached them, we all came to a stop, paralyzed for a moment by their beauty.

"They look too pure to sully with footprints," Sue said softly. The wind had sculpted its own image in the sand, and a few little bird feet had left their marks along the edges, but otherwise the dunes looked untouched, untouchable. An osprey soared above us, heading for the other side, and suddenly I heard the distant *grito* of sea lions. Then, slinging my towel over my shoulder, I headed out over the dunes, making the first human print. The others followed.

From the top of the dunes we looked down onto a tiny cove, even more protected than the wide bay by our camp. About a hundred yards out to sea, a broad rock rose up like a small island above the water's surface. The rock appeared to be heaving, forming and reforming itself in front of my eyes. When I blinked and looked again, I realized that what was heaving was a colony of sea lions, dozens of sleek, muscular animals stretching and sliding and shoving at one another under the morning sun.

We bathed in the calm water of the cove while silver grunion flashed around us, sometimes leaping into the air as if in greeting. Then we stretched out to dry on sun-warmed rocks like our pinniped neighbors.

Later, when the tide had receded beyond the point at the far end of the cove, we walked out around the base of the cliff and wandered down to the next beach. Sue and I gathered shells as we went. Here and there, we came across the bleached bones of a pelican, and once we found coyote tracks heading back toward the dunes. I was digging with my hands in the wet sand by the tide line, looking for clams, when I heard an alien noise. I lifted my head and immediately caught the scent of gasoline. Bob and Carlos, fifty yards ahead of us, had stopped. A car was approaching them from the far end of the beach.

I stood up and wiped my sandy hands on my shorts. Sue tied her straw hat securely under her chin and squared her shoulders. After only twenty-four hours, we had all developed a sense of territoriality, and there was something distinctly unsettling about the sight of an automobile on this virginal beach. The car had stopped, and a man was leaning against the front fender, talking to Bob and Carlos. Sue and I—both of us silent and suspicious—joined them.

The man was small and wiry, about fifty, with gray-blue eyes the color of the sea and an amused smile beneath a neatly trimmed gray mustache. He wore an old navy blue shirt, caked with grease, that looked as though it had once been part of a mechanic's uniform. Across the pocket was sewn the name *Luis*.

"*Buenos días*," Luis greeted us. He touched the brim of his dusty Dodgers cap.

"Luis lives over there," Bob informed us, pointing vaguely down the beach in front of us. I didn't see anything but sand and sea.

Carlos came over and stood next to me. He said nothing, but pointedly shot his eyes toward the 1975 Ford Pinto from which Luis had emerged. I followed Carlos's gaze through glassless windows into the space where the backseat had once been. The space was mostly filled by a spare gas tank, but on the bare metal floor in front of the gas tank, I spotted what Carlos wanted me to see: an ancient, rusty shotgun and a box of shells.

"Did you find any clams?" Luis asked me pleasantly.

"I could see their holes in the sand, but I couldn't dig fast enough to reach them," I admitted.

Luis laughed, and his whole face turned to gold. "You will learn," he said. "I have been here for thirty years, and I have learned many things." He gestured toward the rock island where the sea lions now were all dozing. "I have learned from them."

He turned, leaning his folded forearms against the driver's door of the car. "The *lobos* and the *pelícanos* live on that little island together," he told us. His tone was confidential, as if he were sharing a secret. "In the spring, when the chicks hatch, the *lobos* take great care to avoid the birds' territory. And when the *lobos* have babies, the birds come over and caress them with their beaks. They live together in harmony *porque se respetan*. They respect each other."

Bob was staring at the shotgun, and Luis followed his gaze. "Unfortunately," he smiled, "men do not always have respect like the animals do. Men take babies from the sea before they are big enough to reproduce." I thought with chagrin of the little lobsters and abalone we had accepted willingly. "And some men use the gill nets, even though they are illegal." I remembered Ignacio's dark eyes, wounded and apologetic in his lined face. "So," Luis went on, "at least on my beach, I see to it that the humans and the animals *se respeten*." He removed his cap, smoothed back a mane of tousled gray hair, replaced the cap, and turned to face the sea, arms folded across his chest. His eyes narrowed.

"I have a secret place," he said softly, "where I raise baby abalone. Every day I go to tend them. I keep them safe from the fishermen. I keep them safe from the *lobos*. No one knows where they are. Not even my wife."

"Do you have any children, Don Luis?" Carlos asked. I could tell that he was warming up to the man. "Other than your baby abalone, I mean?"

Luis grinned and slipped into the driver's seat of his car. "Follow me," he said.

The Pinto turned eastward at the far end of the beach and disappeared behind a dune. It was easy enough to follow the tire tracks, however; and after a half-hour walk, we crested the ridge of the beach and emerged at the continuation of the road we had followed to Punta Cono. The same thorny desert scrub was everywhere, and the same rocky desert floor. But across the road, in the shade of an old mesquite, stood the battered black Pinto. Just beyond, a riot of crimson geraniums and untamed tomato vines clustered around a little stone cottage. Above the front door, gleaming in the midday sun, stretched the decorative arch of a white whale rib. Luis waved at us from the side of the house, then disappeared behind it.

Three skinny dogs, one yellow and two black, gave a couple of token barks and then trotted after us, tails wagging. Somewhere, a rooster crowed. Behind the house, a windmill turned lazily in the sea breeze, pumping water from a well. Beds of corn, tomatoes, and squash covered the desert floor. When we came upon Luis, he was crouched beside a woman who knelt in the earth among the green squash leaves. A little boy of about three was chasing chickens across the dirt yard.

For a moment, everything stopped. Luis and the woman stood up, shading their eyes with their hands. The child halted in his tracks and stared. The breeze died, and the windmill stood still.

"*¡Bienvenidos!*" called Luis, and everything came alive again: The windmill revolved, the little boy ran to his grandmother, and she moved toward us, wrapping her hands in her apron and smiling.

"*Leticia Chávez de Castro, a sus órdenes,*" she said, and we all introduced ourselves.

Leti was about the same age as Luis, but her hair was still brown, sun-streaked with gold. Her face was smooth, the color of apricots, and her eyes were sea-foam green. There was an air of serenity about her, as though the calluses on her broad hands had rubbed away all the petty stresses of the world.

On a rough wooden table under a blue plastic awning, a young man was filleting fish. "My son-in-law," Luis told us. "He will prepare the fish for you. Do you like yellowtail?"

"*¡Beto!*" called Leti to her grandson, "bring me a bag full of tomatoes."

We had come back to the front of the house, having wandered through the gardens in the back, and we stood beneath the astonishing whale's rib amid raucous geraniums.

"What beautiful flowers you have, Luis," Sue said.

"A house without a garden is like a house without children," answered Luis, and just as I was thinking about the poetry of rural life, he added with a twinkle, "or like a house without television!"

"Television?" Bob asked, puzzled.

"Well," drawled Luis, "when we visit our daughter and grandchildren in Mexicali, I like to watch TV. It gets lonely here sometimes, you know." He glanced at Leti who rolled her eyes in a gesture understood only by the two of them. "When we have a successful fishing season, I'd like to buy a generator so I can watch videos."

He leaned against the stone wall under the whale rib, his hands in his pockets, regarding us with wry amusement. His eyes, which I had thought were gray, looked as brown as the sun-baked earth. I pictured that old Pinto with its automatic transmission traveling across the desert all the way to Mexicali. I wondered what videos Luis and Leti would watch on winter evenings when the dark descended early and the wind howled up from the sea, drowning out the sound of the surf, the song of the *lobos*.

Over the next few days, we rarely left the little universe of our camp. Life took on the rhythm of the tides, the moon, and the sun. Low tide uncovered the sandbar in the bay, and we, along with flocks of terns and sandpipers, gathered clams. At high tide, rowdy adolescent sea lions went surfing under the stern gaze of their elders. We watched them play in the waves, and we counted noses when they finally heaved themselves back onto the rock, scanning the sea anxiously until the last youngster was safe in the heart of the family again. With the pearly light of dawn we witnessed the mountains emerging, one by one, from the deep belly of Baja, as if the land were creating itself anew. At dusk we cleaned and pounded abalone on the rocks where obstreperous gulls swooped down for scraps and eventually ate from our hands. The twilight seemed to blend the borders between work and play, between man and bird, between light and darkness. When the moon rose late in the evening, we could hear the *lobos* singing across the silver dunes.

The night before our departure I dreamed that the granite cone on the point was a volcano. Its body heaved and glowed with living fire, and I was standing in the light, holding a newborn infant in my arms.

From my sleeping bag the next morning, I whispered, "Carlos, let's stay here forever."

"Mmmm," he answered drowsily.

"Carlos," I said again, "last night I dreamed we had a baby son."

"Mmm-hmmm," Carlos said, and he pulled me to him. I lay still. Beyond the tent window, squadrons of pelicans skimmed the bay, soft and rosy with dawn. I thought of how far I had journeyed in the years since my desert nightmare of birthing a twisted monster, and I marveled at the undreamed-of *caminos* I had traveled in those years.

As we left the coastal ridge and descended back into the desert from which we had come, I recalled Father Baegert's acrid description of the "waterless, thornful rock sticking up between two oceans." But then there came to me, rumbling up from the depths of Baja, the words of Octavio Paz, Mexico's great poet:

El mundo tiene playas todavía   The world still has beaches
y un barco allá te espera, siempre.   and out there a boat awaits you, always.

La Sierra de San Francisco

Gracias a la vida	Thanks to life
que me ha dada tanto:	that has given me so much:
me ha dado la marcha de mis pies cansados	the march of my weary feet
con ellos anduve ciudades y charcos,	through cities and across ponds,
playas y desiertos, montañas y llanos	beaches, deserts, mountains, plains
y la casa tuya, tu calle y tu patio.	your house, your road, and your patio.

—Violeta Parra, "Gracias a la Vida"

I n the end, it was a journey of inches. I had this thought while clinging to the back of an aged mule who was picking his way, stone by stone and inch by inch, down a precipitous canyon trail somewhere deep in the heart of Baja's Sierra de San Francisco. It was April 1993, two weeks before my fiftieth birthday, and we had come to the mountains to see the famous cave paintings, ancient art left by a vanished race. We had arrived at that particular canyon trail, that particular moment, through a long and gradual process.

Crossing the desert had been the first step. When we set out from home, the Shaffers' daughter Linda, now a college graduate with a degree in archaeology, rode along with Carlos and me, occupying the back seat of our Isuzu Trooper. Bob and Sue followed behind in their Explorer.

As we began to descend from the cool springs and blue palms of Cataviña into the Vizcaíno Desert, I turned in my seat and told Linda, "Prepare yourself for a long, boring ride between here and San Ignacio. This part of the trip is pretty desolate."

But the previous winter's rains had ended long years of drought, and every dormant seed that had harbored its secret life throughout those long years was now blazing with energy. Everything that could bloom was blooming, and the desert floor was a brilliant carpet of green and gold, mauve and magenta. The air pulsed with fragrance, hummed with the voices of a million insects. Even the fences, built with living yucca stalks, had sprouted leaves.

"When does the boring part begin?" Linda asked, her head stretched eagerly through the open window. I laughed. It was hard to believe that this was the arid wasteland in which so many men had perished in the course of Baja's long history.

"It's a lot less bleak than I remember it," I told her. "In fact, it's a whole different world than I remember!"

Linda pulled her head back into the car and leaned her chin affectionately on my shoulder like a big golden retriever. "It *is* a whole new world, Aunt Judy," she grinned. "You're not getting old on me, are you?"

The next step was to arrange for the burros and mules and guides we would need for a cave painting expedition. Such arrangements, we had been told, could be made in San Ignacio. When we arrived in town, we headed for Oscar Fischer's Motel La Posada, sure that Oscar could advise us. But at the Posada we were greeted by Oscar's son, now a handsome young man.

"My father is not in," he told us cordially. "Can I help you?"

We rented two rooms for the night. I sat down on the edge of a dingy army-green bedspread which covered a thin mattress. Yellow paint peeled from the walls. The room's only adornment was one bare lightbulb protruding from the wall opposite the bed.

"I forgot how shabby this place is," I said to Carlos.

Carlos had removed one of his thongs and was standing on the closed toilet lid in the bathroom, the rubber sandal poised over his head like a club.

"That *pinche* mosquito is going to keep us awake all night," he muttered.

"Has the Posada changed or have I changed?" I asked, not even sure he could hear me. There was a *splat* from the bathroom.

"Shit!" Carlos hissed. "I missed the son of a bitch."

A wave of fatigue swept over me. I stretched out on the lumpy bed and stared at the stained ceiling. I didn't think I could face another mountain, another spine-jarring dirt road. I didn't want to get on a mule; I suddenly remembered that I had always been terrified of horses. I didn't want to spend a single night on this sagging mattress in this depressing room.

"Carlos," I whispered to the empty air, "am I getting old?"

I heard another slap of rubber against the bathroom wall and Carlos's triumphant chortle. Then he came into the bedroom and sat down beside me on the bed.

"I got him," he announced.

I closed my eyes, too weary to respond. *It was a silly question anyway,* I thought to myself. *Of course I'm getting old; I'm going to be fifty.*

Carlos took my hand. "The *pitahaya dulce* is the sweetest fruit in all of Baja California," he said, "maybe even in all of Mexico. The *indígenas* used to measure the seasons of the year by the seasons of the *pitahaya.*"

I pulled my hand away and turned on my side, my back to Carlos. I wasn't in the mood for a history lesson.

"But," Carlos went on, "they knew that, until it has opened completely, the *pitahaya* is bitter and harsh. So they waited patiently for the fruit to mature, because only then does it achieve its perfection."

He lay down, fitting his body against mine and wrapping his arm around me. "It was worth the wait," he said.

Later, we all walked down to the plaza. San Ignacio had undergone a few superficial changes, but its soul remained untouched. Jacaranda trees in full flower arched over a narrow lane lined by earthen walls painted in vivid blues and yellows. The new satellite dish beside the old mission church was hardly visible, hidden behind a cascade of deep pink bougainvillea; and the new video rental store, apparently the most popular hangout in town for teenagers, had not yet snared the smaller children who still scampered up and down the steps of the gazebo in the plaza.

It was in the plaza that we came across Oscar. He was sitting on one of the benches in the shade of a laurel tree, his face as faded as the old baseball cap pulled low over his eyes. At first, none of us recognized him.

"*Buenas tardes,*" he called out softly.

"*¡Señor Fischer!*" Carlos exclaimed. He pronounced it "Fee-share."

"Did my boy take care of you?" Oscar asked vaguely. He suddenly seemed just another old man there on the bench among all the other old men of the town.

"Yes, Oscar," Sue answered. "We're staying the night at La Posada."

"Are you retired now, my friend?" Carlos took a seat beside Oscar. Out of nowhere, a box of dominoes appeared between them. The old twinkle glinted for a moment in Oscar's pale blue eyes.

"I have more time now to practice my game," he replied, and he started to deal.

"Later, dude!" Linda called to Carlos, and the rest of us turned and headed across the plaza to a new *lonchería* that stood where the date stand used to be, leaving Carlos to conduct business in the time-honored way of San Ignacio.

Reaching the village of San Francisco de la Sierra was the third step. We were to meet our guides there and load our equipment onto burros before continuing by mule into the remote canyons that held the fabled caves. We left San Ignacio after an early breakfast, and thirty minutes later we turned onto a dirt road that headed east into the mountains. For the first few miles, the road ascended gently, winding through verdant desert where ocotillos waved red-tipped fingers in a gay springtime greeting. Carlos drove with a half smile on his face, his left elbow resting on the edge of the open window. Linda and I compared notes on what we had read about rock art.

In the Sonoran Desert, from Arizona through southern California and well into the northern regions of Baja, countless caves enfold the mysterious art of generations past. Most of this rock art is abstract, consisting primarily of geometric designs: spirals and sunbursts and undulating lines. I had seen such paintings in San Diego's Anza-Borrego Desert, and I had seen them on the giant boulders near Cataviña, almost five hundred miles from Anza-Borrego. Despite the distance, it was easy to believe what the anthropologists say—that these vibrant, mysterious patterns are the work of a single culture, for the styles are the same. The few hundred Indian families who still remain in northern Baja speak a language that closely resembles that of the Kumeyaay people of southern California. The white man's border is not of their making, and the Indians, at least, have never forgotten that they are all one family.

But in the southern half of the Baja peninsula, deep within the mountains that rise from the desert floor, a different style of rock art illuminates the walls of ancient caves. These murals, painted on high ceilings and broad rock walls, are clearly the work of another culture. Unlike the artists of the Sonoran Desert, the muralists created figures: towering men and women, prancing mountain sheep and antelope, rabbits, and soaring birds, and whales. No one knows who these muralists were or when they lived. No one knows how or why they painted, nor the meaning behind their work. No one knows why they vanished or where they went. But no one who encounters them is ever quite the same again.

The Cochimí Indians, who lived in the land of the cave paintings at the time of the missionaries, told the Jesuits that long before, during the time of legend, a race of giants had come down from the north into the Cochimí country. It was these giants, they claimed, whose images glowed from the high ceilings and unreachable walls of mountain caves.

"But some people believe," Linda explained, "that the Cochimí themselves were the artists. They may not have wanted the padres to know that they were continuing to practice their own sacred rituals, their own religion. They may have just invented the tale of an earlier people in order to protect themselves."

"I can believe that," Carlos remarked.

"I like the race-of-giants theory better," I mused. "It makes a great story."

We all fell silent, having exhausted the scanty information available in books on the subject of the origin of the cave paintings. The air shimmered with sunshine and new life. Two coyote pups pranced across the road and disappeared in a forest of *cardón* cactus. Serene and regal, the rows of *cardones* stretched away to the misty horizon like ancient guardians of the land, like the living spirits of a vanished race of giants.

As the road climbed, it narrowed, and as it narrowed, it deteriorated. Once we had to stop and gather rocks to fill in ruts too deep to navigate. While we were rebuilding the road, a herd of goats came ambling down the hillside in front of us, bells clinking softly. Many were babies, their spindly legs still wobbly as they trotted after their mothers. Close behind the goats came their keeper, a boy of about ten who leaped from rock to rock as if he were one of the herd. Instead of the shepherd's staff of storybooks, he carried the instrument of a modern goatherd: a pair of battered binoculars.

After a time, signs of human habitation began to appear. We passed a ranch where the family's laundry dried in the sun, spread across a stand of nopal cactus. We passed an old man repairing his *tinaja,* a large stone cistern for collecting and storing water. We came face-to-face with a battered pickup truck heading down the mountain, its bed overflowing with teenagers in cowboy hats who waved cheerfully as the truck pulled over into the thorny chaparral to let us pass.

The village of San Francisco de la Sierra was only a little cluster of shacks on a high desert mesa. We arrived without drama; the road simply disappeared into the dusty earth, and we were there. A woman was stirring something in a black pot over a wood fire beside a hut of plywood and tar paper. Two toddlers played in the dirt at her feet.

"Excuse me, *señora,*" Carlos called out. "Can you tell me where we might find Señor Enrique Arce?"

The woman turned and pointed with her wooden spoon. "*Allá en la casita blanca,*" she replied. "Over there in the little white house."

Oscar had explained that, to protect the caves, the Mexican government had prohibited any tourism there without officially sanctioned guides. Mr. Arce, San Francisco's government delegate, had been expecting us, having been radioed the day before by Oscar.

"What took you so long?" he boomed amicably, after we all made our formal introductions. "Your guides have been waiting for you since first light! The day is half gone. *¡Vámonos!*"

Mr. Arce, a corpulent, leather-faced man of about forty, mounted a chestnut mule and indicated that we should follow with our vehicles. We wound through the trackless desert for half a mile before coming to a stop in Rancho Palo Verde, a settlement even smaller than San Francisco de la Sierra.

Five or six wooden houses, all painted in bright colors and adorned by multihued flowers, clustered in a rough circle around a central yard of packed dirt. A leafy palo verde tree shaded a corner of this communal yard, and five mules, heads hanging low in patient endurance, clustered around the tree. Sitting on the ground and resting against the tree's thick trunk were two figures who scrambled to their feet at our arrival.

"Your guides," announced Mr. Arce, and my first thought was: *Why, one of them is a woman!*

"*Yo soy Juan Pablo,*" said the smaller of the two guides, a very young man with a thick black beard and warm golden eyes.

The other guide, beardless and soft-skinned as a woman but broad shouldered and tall, extended a hand shyly and said, in a voice neither masculine nor feminine, "*Me llamo Jesús María. Todos me dicen Chema.*"

We shook hands all around, Mr. Arce took his leave, and we began unloading the cars. Juan Pablo and Chema ran across the little central clearing and disappeared behind one of the houses, reappearing in a moment with a train of four burros.

Sue nudged me as we piled up sleeping bags and tents. "Is Chema a man or a woman?" she whispered.

"Good question," I answered. "The name's a man's name. But did you feel his—I mean her—skin when we shook hands?"

"Really soft," said Linda, who had come up beside us with a duffel bag full of cooking equipment. "Do you think maybe it's just a very young male?"

Sue said, "Doesn't look like any young male I've ever seen."

"Actually," I observed, "I don't think I could guess Chema's age any better than I could guess the gender. Could be anywhere from eighteen to forty!"

"Well, we're going to have to choose a pronoun," Linda declared. "I'm not going to refer to our head guide as *it* for the whole trip!"

"How do you know who's the head guide?" Sue asked.

"Just look," Linda replied, and we all sat down on the pile of sleeping bags and watched Juan Pablo and Chema work.

They were packing all our camping equipment, item by item, into small plastic crates. When they had filled the crates, they covered each one with goatskin. Then they strapped the crates to the burros, balancing two crates of equal weight across the back of each beast and cinching them tightly with a leather strap.

Linda was right. Chema was clearly in charge, checking Juan Pablo's work carefully, re-balancing a crate here or adjusting a strap there.

Several of the village children buzzed around Chema like little drag-
onflies, watching the whole process in open admiration.

"He moves like a man," Sue whispered. Chema had a foot planted
firmly against the flank of one of the burros and was leaning back,
pulling a strap with both hands.

"Or like a '90s woman," Linda said. "He's incredibly strong."

"Looks like we've settled on the pronoun," I observed. "Whatever
the anatomy is, this person identifies as a man, functions as a man.
We're all using *he*."

"I'm comfortable with that," Sue agreed, "but I'm still curious."

Finally, we were ready to depart.

"*¡Híjole!*" exclaimed Carlos, "I can't believe how much stuff we
brought."

"It's downright embarrassing," Bob agreed.

Our guides had not been able to fit everything onto four burros
and had borrowed a fifth burro from one of the villagers at the last
minute. They were both sweating profusely from the exertion of preparing five *norteamericanos* for three days in the mountains. Chema
and Juan Pablo each carried one wool serape and a bit of dried meat
slipped beneath the mule's saddle blanket.

The burros were sagging with their loads. A little girl ran across
the dirt to where Chema stood in the shade and handed him a bundle
of still-steaming tortillas wrapped in a blue-and-white checkered towel.
He picked her up and kissed her cheek, then set her down gently. She
clung to his hand, and the children who had been following Chema
around gathered expectantly under the tree.

Juan Pablo led the mules out one by one, he and Chema having
decided in advance who would ride which animal. He introduced us
each to our mule by name and helped us mount.

"*Macho Viejo*," he told me as he cupped his two hands to boost
me to the stirrup. "He is very old but he is very wise."

I chuckled. "Now I have two *machos viejos*," I joked, and my own
bravado made me feel a little better. I swung my right leg over the
mule's back and settled into the saddle. "Well, mule," I said softly, "it's
going to be you and me, baby."

We left in single file, Chema in front and Juan Pablo, along with the burro train, bringing up the rear. Chema's little fan club followed us to the edge of the village where they stood watching until we were out of sight.

We moved slowly across the mesa, leaving the settlement behind. A red-tailed hawk swooped and dove over the canyon before us, its tail glowing russet in the sun. The bells around the burros' necks made a soft *clink-clink* as the little beasts picked their way through the chaparral. I settled into an easy rhythm on Macho Viejo's back, absorbing the warmth of his strong animal body and the strangely sweet fragrance of his sweat. The old mule seemed utterly calm and confident, and I felt my fear drifting away into the sage-scented desert air.

The trail dipped into an arroyo where a gnarled old pepper tree leaned across a chain-link fence. Behind the fence was what I first thought to be another little village. Three or four tiny cement-block houses were scattered over a low hill. Spiny cholla cactus crept across the earth between them.

"*Aquí están mis abuelos,*" Chema said, pulling his mule to a stop. "My grandparents are here." Then I saw the crosses on top of the little houselike structures.

"It's a cemetery!" Bob dismounted, rubbing his buttocks and stretching his back from side to side.

"Sore already, Dad?" Linda called out gaily.

"Is your family all from around here, Chema?" Carlos asked in Spanish.

"Everyone in Rancho Palo Verde is my family," Chema answered, "my parents and my sisters and brothers and all their children. And my grandparents and great grandparents are right here."

Juan Pablo rode up to Chema and said something I couldn't hear. Then he galloped away toward the far edge of the mesa, leaving the rest of us in the pepper tree's shade. Chema yelled once at the burros to establish his authority, then turned to Carlos.

"Juan Pablo is going to check *la bajada,* the descent," he said. "It is sometimes very bad, and we haven't gone down for over a month. I want him to see whether it is safe for the mules."

At his words, the cold fist of fear that had floated so gently away gripped my chest again. I took a deep breath and thought suddenly of

Doña Josefina, now four years dead, her calm face and deep, wise eyes floating in the air before me.

Sue was riding toward me. Swaying majestically astride her mule in her wide-brimmed hat and red neck bandanna, she looked like a pioneer woman.

"These guys are real *californios*," she observed. "Did you hear Chema talking about his family? I bet they've been here since the days of the padres."

I knew what she meant. For Christmas, Sue and Bob had given Carlos and me a copy of Harry Crosby's *The Last of the Californios,* and all four of us had poured over it during several communal dinners before our trip.

The Jesuit fathers had arrived in Baja with small retinues from Europe consisting mostly of soldiers and a few craftsmen. The entire peninsula was claimed as part of New Spain, so the Spanish kings felt justified in bestowing California land upon whomever they chose. When the Jesuits left the New World, their followers—the soldiers who had guarded them, the craftsmen who had labored for them— were given land grants in Baja's rugged mountains. Many of these land grants were the same *rancherías* where the indigenous people already lived, taking advantage of the few available water sources. Intermarriage had been commonplace for decades, and within a few generations the new *californios* were raising cattle and goats, harvesting grapes and oranges, mangos and figs, and bringing forth a new culture deep in the heart of the peninsula.

Because of the isolation of these remote mountain communities, the settlements had remained almost untouched by time. Their men and women were still living much as they lived in the eighteenth century, a hearty, self-sufficient people bearing, perhaps, in their collective unconscious, a distant memory of the ancient gods.

Bob had hobbled over and was listening to our conversation. "Take a look at Chema's shoes," he said, "and Juan Pablo's chaps. They're homemade, out of goatskin. These guys are something!" He shook his head admiringly. "They tan their own leather, they make their own cheese . . . ."

"Yeah," agreed Linda, who had been putting her mule through its paces and was now leaning on its neck affectionately. "And they're awesome with their animals."

"Sure," Carlos pointed out, coming up beside Linda, "their animals are the most valuable possessions they have. Can't use a car here. But a good mule . . . ."

" . . . is better than a good woman," I interrupted. "Chema's more worried about the mules than about us!"

"Gringos come . . . and gringos go," Carlos grinned. "Mules are family! Here's Juan Pablo now."

When I saw *la bajada,* even the spirit of Doña Josefina couldn't stem the tide of panic that engulfed me. We all gathered at the edge of the mesa, contemplating the descent before us.

The trail was no more than a foot wide. It was unbelievably steep, almost ninety degrees in some spots, and strewn with loose, rocky soil. Its sickening hairpin curves wound down and down the side of the canyon wall for a distance I judged to be well over a thousand feet. Far below, we could see the glint of water and the tops of palm trees.

"*Está muy mala la bajada, Yudy,*" said Juan Pablo softly. He addressed us all by name: I was Yudy, Sue was Susana, and Bob was Roberto. Linda and Carlos needed no translation.

I tried to give him a smile. There was something tender about Juan Pablo, a gentleness that reminded me of my own children. He was a newlywed, we had learned, and was building a house for his bride in his own ranch, three hours away by mule. As Macho Viejo obediently started down the precipitous trail, I wondered if Juan Pablo's young wife would ever see him again.

Slowly we inched our way into the canyon. After a time, my terror simply disappeared, along with the whole rest of the world. Nothing existed but the next stone, the next step. I turned everything over to Macho Viejo who seemed to have understood, long before I did, that no journey is impossible. He never balked, and he never faltered, although he would often stop for a moment at the edge of a particularly perilous section of the trail as if considering which of several choices was the best. In the end, he always found the firmest rock on which to place his hoof and the smoothest path around a precipitous drop. I began to feel a profound affection for the creature and a deep respect for his wisdom.

The trail leveled out briefly, and Chema, in the lead, reined up his mule beneath a wild fig tree that clung to the cliff wall. We all stopped while Juan Pablo and Chema conferred. Then Chema signaled to Carlos, who dismounted and went over to the two guides. When Carlos turned to the rest of us, he had a bemused expression on his face.

"It seems we're coming to a stretch of slick rock," he said. "It's too slippery for the animals to carry riders. They want us to get down and walk. They want us to lead our mules until we get to the dirt trail again."

I waited for terror to strike. The cliff ledge was as narrow as ever, and I couldn't even see the bottom of the canyon from where we were. I hadn't expected to have to trust my own feet, and I certainly hadn't expected to lead a mule. But somehow, as I swung down from Macho Viejo and slipped the reins over his head, I felt no fear. There was a voice in my head that I didn't recognize, and it didn't even occur to me to wonder whose voice it was or where it came from. The voice said, "Think like a mule."

There were a few intense moments when I thought that Macho Viejo was going to slide right into me, sending us both into the abyss. But I kept my focus on the next step and then the next, trying to sense the terrain with whatever part of my being I shared with the animal who plodded along behind me, his life literally in my hands. When we finally found the dirt trail again, and Chema signaled us to remount, I buried my face in the mule's warm neck and caressed his shaggy mane. He just stood there, patient and stolid, waiting to carry me away.

Even before I saw the grapevines and the olive trees, even before I caught the scent of orange blossoms drifting up the valley, I knew we had come to the canyon floor when Juan Pablo began to whistle. His light, melodious tune was like a trail of music leading us down the last stony stretch of *la bajada* and into the Garden of Eden below.

"Santa Teresa," Chema announced, gesturing toward the tiny village hidden behind a large screen of palm trees, "and *las huertas,* the orchards."

We were riding along the banks of a little stream that watered the fruit trees and vines of Santa Teresa. Everyone was slightly giddy, partly with relief at our safe arrival and partly with amazement at the enchanted world in which we had landed. Bob began to sing "Don't Fence Me In," and the rest of us joined the chorus. When the song ended, Juan Pablo took up the tune in a clear whistle, never missing a note.

It was getting late, and although we were not far from our destination, our guides insisted that we camp for the night outside of Santa Teresa. When we had dismounted, both Chema and Juan Pablo stretched out on their bellies by the stream and sucked in great gulps of water, along with the mules and burros. The rest of us sipped daintily from our Evian bottles before we set about making camp.

While we were cooking dinner, a couple of ranchers from Santa Teresa appeared on the opposite bank. Chema and Juan Pablo crossed over to talk with them, and Bob, under the pretext of gathering more wood for the fire, followed a few minutes later.

"Juan Pablo was bargaining with those guys for some palm fronds for the house he's building," he told us when he returned. "Three burro loads of palm fronds for one goat and a kilo of cheese."

"Imagine," Sue said, "they don't even need money here!"

"What's even more amazing," Bob went on, "is that, when they didn't think I was listening, they weren't speaking Spanish to each other."

"What were they speaking?" I asked, pouring pasta into a pot of almost-boiling water.

"I didn't recognize the language. I think it was probably an Indian dialect. But they obviously didn't want me to hear it."

Linda remarked, "That supports the Cochimí-as-muralist theory. Maybe these guys have maintained their culture more than any of us know. They've just kept it hidden from the white man."

"Speak for yourself, paleface," Carlos laughed, tossing her an orange he had plucked from one of the trees as we rode by.

Chema and Juan Pablo were up at dawn the next day. Before we had even brewed our coffee, they had the animals packed and saddled and ready to go, and we were on the trail before the dew had dried.

Compared to the previous day's trip, the final descent to the valley of the caves was easy. We were all in high spirits as we wound down the canyon wall, palm trees and river appearing and disappearing with the trail's twisting curves. When we were just a hundred feet or so above the floor, Chema called out, casually, "*Allá está La Cueva Pintada.*"

"Oh my God!" cried Linda. "Look!"

Across a narrow canyon, like a proscenium carved into the rock, a broad, shallow cave opened up. Clearly visible, and utterly astonishing in this remote place, were scores of painted figures covering the back wall of the cave. We could not make out the details, but there was an immediate sense of motion, of living energy, that emanated from the figures, although they were half hidden in the shadows. My heart was still pounding when we came to a stop on the canyon floor by the rocky bank of the river.

"This is your kitchen," Chema announced, indicating a group of flat boulders, "and there," pointing to a sandy area across the stream, "is your bedroom."

While our guides unpacked and hobbled the animals, we set up our tents. The sun was hot; by the time we finished, we were all sweating and streaked with dust. Thirty yards downstream, the river cascaded into a shallow pool surrounded by smooth rocks and thick foliage. Linda was the first to find it, and she had already stripped off her clothes and was lolling in the water by the time the rest of us arrived.

"Oh man," she murmured, "don't wake me up!"

"Don Carlos," called Chema, "don't you want to go see the caves?"

"*Al rato,*" Carlos called back. "In a little while!"

Then we were all stripping and splashing into the pool, to the bewildered amusement of the guides who stretched out on the flat rocks of the "kitchen" for a siesta while they awaited their inscrutable charges.

That afternoon we all hiked to Painted Cave. In his homemade goatskin shoes, Chema fairly flew over the rocks, while the rest of us, plodding behind in our expensive Hi-Tec boots, puffed and whined and crawled our way up the cliff. I regretted the little day pack I had on my back; it seemed to grow heavier and heavier as I climbed. With what I had thought was prudent planning, I had filled it with a bottle of water, a snakebite kit, a couple of Granola bars, and a tube of sunscreen. But Juan Pablo, who slowed his own pace to keep an eye on the rest of us, showed me how to make a spout from a palm leaf to catch the water from a tiny seep in the rock; and he showed me the *ojocote* beans that the natives used for snakebite. Once he pointed out puma tracks, and once he stopped, listening to a faint bird call which he identified with a grin of delight as that of a *cardenal,* the locals' name for the red cardinal.

The energy that we had sensed dimly across the canyon on our first glimpse of Painted Cave, those emanations of movement and life, were dizzying at close range. They swarmed around us and above us: towering human figures with arms upraised in blessing or in eternal surprise; herds of deer in flight, their graceful necks extended, legs reaching for the next step, mouths open to the next breath. Bighorn sheep ascended the wall of the cave, their massive chests undiminished by the centuries. Two condors rose up together, wings and talons spread wide, heads stretched toward some distant heaven. A couple of fishlike figures seemed to swim across the rock, and what seemed like a huge whale made its endless way to the surface of an endless sea.

The mural was painted in shades of red and black, some of the human figures bicolored and bisected. *Was that symbolic of some ancient androgynous state,* I wondered, *and was Chema a living example?* Many of the figures, both human and animal, were superimposed on one another in a manner reminiscent of the spatial rearrangements "invented" by European Cubists. With just a few skillful lines, the cave artists had managed to represent the intimate relationships between individuals and among groups, the creatures of the air and of the water, the bipeds and the quadrupeds of the earth. And informing it all, like the wind that ruffled the tops of the palm trees far below us, was an ineffable spirit. It seemed to rise from the headdresses and raised fingertips of the human figures; it seemed to flow from the mouths of the sheep and the deer, and to lift the birds' wings and the whale's flippers. It seemed to embrace us all. We spoke in whispers and trod softly, as though we were moving over hallowed ground.

That night around the fire, we considered the various theories of the meaning behind the paintings. Were they the work of priests, the center of some religious ritual? Were they a spiritual preparation for the hunt, or a kind of schoolroom for the young? Were they the illustrations that accompanied a tribe's storyteller? All of the above? Or something far beyond our limited imaginations?

Sue favored the schoolroom theory, and Bob thought it all had something to do with hunting. Linda leaned toward a ritual/spiritual explanation. Carlos suggested that perhaps it was simply an ancient form of graffiti, spray-painted on the caves by a bygone gang.

"You've been working in the barrio too long, Carlos!" I laughed.

"What do you think, Chema?" Sue asked.

Juan Pablo had brewed a tea he called *té de venado*, deer tea, from an herb he had gathered on our way back from the cave. Now Chema sipped from his steaming cup and smiled shyly at Sue who was slicing an orange with her Swiss army knife.

"How much would a knife like that cost?" he asked. "As much as a used pickup?"

That night, after the crickets had stopped singing, I dreamed of *La Cueva Pintada*. A group of people was gathered on the floor of the cave—men, women, and children clustered around a small campfire. Some were carving on wooden branches with knifelike instruments, and some were weaving reeds into baskets. Some were just reclining in the warm glow and talking softly among themselves. In the firelight, their long shadows moved languidly on the wall of the cave against the painted figures. And then, as the light flickered over the rock wall, the painted figures themselves began to stretch and to move, dancing and bending among the living shadows until the whole cave was alive with movement, animals and men and fire and rock all merging together in a golden glow.

Over the next few days we hiked to other caves and explored other murals. Linda found arrowheads, which she carefully photographed and replaced, and bits of obsidian which, as she explained, must have been brought from distant places and were evidence of widespread trade. Sue discovered several *metates*, flat rocks with deep depressions worn into them by the grinding stones of long-vanished chefs. Bob spotted an orange tanager, and Carlos found mountain lion tracks. I learned to tell time by sound: the low cooing of doves at dawn, the chorus of frogs at dark. All of us became lighter and lighter, gradually shedding our backpacks, our heavy boots, our useless Evian water bottles.

The night before our departure I awoke sometime between frogs and doves. Restless, I crawled out of the tent and crept up to a rocky ledge above our camp. Across from where I sat, the canyon wall glowed silver, and on the canyon's rim, almost two thousand feet above me, a full moon bloomed like an enchanted flower.

As the moon rose higher, the whole valley filled with silver light. It spangled the tips of palm leaves and shimmered over river water. It reflected off the rocky cliffs like music, echoing through distant caves and back down canyons and arroyos.

After a while, among the ghostly moonlight echoes, I began to discern voices. They filtered through the pale light, carrying with them the warmth of the earth. There was Miguel Sevillano's soft hum as he caressed a newly-polished guitar, and there was Gilberto's song from deep in some southern California canyon. There was Juan Pablo's bright whistle as he rode into Santa Teresa and Oscar's faded voice recounting old times. There was Señora Duarte's gentle "*buenas noches*" and Luis's hearty "*bienvenidos*;" there was Doña Josefina's laugh—sharp as desert air—and Rosa's sweet soprano. There was Ignacio's shy greeting, the patient murmurings of Encarnación and little Esperanza, and El Anima's wild call.

And as I listened, the voices grew stronger, pouring down from the rocks and up from the river, overflowing the canyon and filling the night. Then I heard my voice join with the others, the sounds all intertwining and blending into one rich melody, one song, until at last I no longer knew where their stories ended and my own began.

Epilogue

I returned from the Sierra de San Francisco in April 1993, only a few months before the twentieth anniversary of the completion of Baja's transpeninsular highway. At the time, I was too dazzled by that transcendent spring to notice anything else; but had I looked around with objective eyes, I would have understood the magnitude of the changes wrought over the two decades of the highway's existence.

Tourism has been steadily growing over the years and has virtually exploded since 1993. The increasing traffic along Mexico Highway 1 is straining the resources of villages ill-equipped to handle crowds. Rampant construction has utterly transformed the environment in many popular vacation spots; graffiti has appeared on every available surface along the roadside.

But crucial as it has been to the peninsula's evolution, Highway 1 has not been the sole agent of change. Mexico itself leaped into a new era during the early 1990s, and Baja led the way.

The North American Free Trade Agreement, signed in January 1994, catapulted Baja California into a brawling international marketplace. Two months later Tijuana's streets erupted with violence when Luis Donaldo Colosio (the PRI's popular presidential candidate) fell to an assassin's bullet. In December of that year, the peso crashed, and all of Mexico reeled.

Since then, Tijuana's shantytowns have swollen more than ever with the human flood pouring northward in a desperate bid for survival, while in the other California, Anglos and Latinos eye each other suspiciously across a widening abyss of fear and misunderstanding. The border has become a zone of constant danger for both immigrants and guards. And deep in the heart of Baja, by the ancient boulders of Cataviña, uniformed soldiers patrol the wilderness with M16 rifles, seeking out drug smugglers who drop like locusts from the night sky.

And yet . . . And yet, to the red-tailed hawk soaring across vast desert silences, very little in Baja has changed. Beyond the thin swath cut by Highway 1 and its tributaries, thousands of square miles of wild country still remain: sweep of beach and shadow of mountain and the voice of the old gods in the wind. This splendid peninsula will prevail. Having survived *conquistadores* and missionaries, pirates and soldiers of fortune, Baja will survive the twentieth century as well.

Early this year, in a roadside restaurant, I came face to face with Baja's indomitable spirit. He was a tall young man eating *machaca* at a wooden table. His shoulder-length black hair reminded me of a raven's wing.

"*Soy Cochimí*," he announced. I informed him that according to all my books, there were no Cochimí left. He laughed, a long, hearty laugh like water on desert stones. Then he started naming all the surrounding mountains. "The Place Where the Rock Weeps," he translated, and "The Place Where the Hawk Flies." When he had finished his lunch he drove off in a pickup truck and disappeared into The Place Where the Sun Sleeps.

I thought of him a week later at Laguna San Ignacio where we had come to see the gray whales and their calves. Our host during our stay was Josele Varela, a marine biologist from Mexico City who runs a self-proclaimed eco-camp on the shores of the lagoon. His establishment, which he calls *Kuyima*, has emerged with the new Baja, one of a handful of such far-flung outposts dedicated to preserving a besieged environment.

On this morning, Josele was explaining the curious name he had chosen for his enterprise.

"*Kuyima* is a Cochimí word," he said. "It's the name we gave to one of the whales who visited us our first year here. She was especially friendly and would raise herself high into the air when she saw our boat. We called her Kuyima, She Who Dances in Clouds." Then he turned and gazed across that fertile bay, alive with the breathing of whales and the hum of birds' wings. We were all keenly aware of the commercial pressures to build a salt plant there. When Josele spoke again he seemed shy, an outdoorsman ill at ease with words. "*Kuyima* has another translation," he said softly. "It also means *luz en la oscuridad*, light in the darkness."

May it be so. *Que así sea.*

> Judy Goldstein Botello
> Escondido, California
> April, 1998

Other Baja California Titles from Sunbelt Publications

The Cave Paintings of Baja California
by Harry W. Crosby
0-932653-23-5 $39.95
A full-color account of the great murals of an unknown people. Depicts the author's discovery and documentation of a world-class archaeological region in remote central Baja California.

Backroad Baja: The Central Region
Tom and Patti Higginbotham
0-9632222-3-6 $14.95
This guide details 20 backcountry trips to beaches, missions, ranches, and the Indian rock art sites of central Baja California. Includes maps, logs, and trip information.

Bicycling Baja
By Bonnie Wong
0-932653-04-9 $12.95
Whether it's a long excursion along Mexico 1 from Tijuana to Cabo San Lucas, or a day-ride near the border, *Bicycling Baja* is for cyclists who enjoy a challenge.

Also available from Sunbelt Publications:

Dawson's Baja California Travel Series
by Dawson's Bookshop
This series recounts various personal narratives of travel and adventure from the earliest times to the present. Only 21 of the 51 volumes originally published remain available. Please contact us for a complete list of these rare and unique and out-of-print books.

For a company catalog, please contact us at:

Sunbelt Publications
1250 Fayette Street
El Cajon, CA 92020
619-258-4911 or 800-626-6579 (orders only)